D1569169

THE LOST LEGACY
OF MUHAMMAD ALI

THE LOST LEGACY OF MUHAMMAD ALI

Thomas Hauser

www.sportclassicbooks.com

Published in the United States of America by Sport Media Publishing Inc.,
Wilmington, Delaware, and simultaneously in Canada.

For information about permission to reproduce selections from this book, please
write to:
Permissions
Sport Media Publishing, Inc.,
21 Carlaw Ave.,
Toronto, Ontario, Canada, M4M 2R6
www.sportclassicbooks.com

Cover design: Paul Hodgson
Front Cover Photographs: The SPORT Collection (main), Alicia Shulman (inset)
Back Cover Photograph: The SPORT Collection
Interior Photographs: All courtesy The SPORT Collection, except pp. 1, 3, 13, 71,
    129, 191, 192 Alicia Shulman
Interior design: Greg Oliver
This book is set in Bembo.

ISBN: 1-894963-46-6

Library of Congress Cataloging-in-Publication Data

Hauser, Thomas.
  The lost legacy of Muhammad Ali / by Thomas Hauser.
    p. cm.
  Includes index.
  ISBN 1-894963-46-6 (hardcover)
  1. Ali, Muhammad, 1942- 2. Boxers (Sports)—United States—Biography. I. Title.

  GV1132.A4H38 2005
  796.83'092—dc22

                                                                    2005013725
Printed in Canada

Muhammad Ali belongs to the world.
This book is dedicated to everyone who is part of his story.

TABLE OF CONTENTS

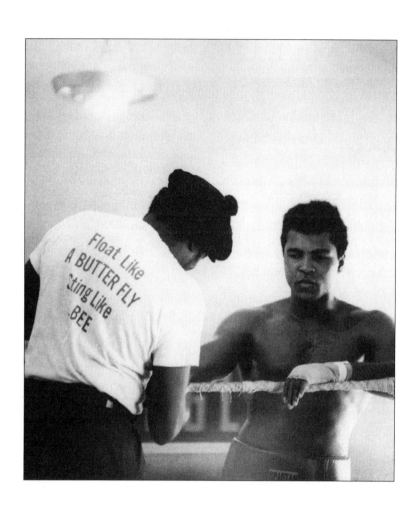

The Reasons for
This Book

Fourteen years ago, in the preface to *Muhammad Ali: His Life and Times*, I wrote, "Even as the Ali chronicles grow, new generations are born; and to them, Ali is more legend than reality, part of America's distant past."

Those words are even more true today than in 1991.

Ali was, and still is, a transcendental figure in American life. But in recent years, he has been packaged and repackaged, and the reasons for his importance as well as the electrifying nature of his persona have been obscured in a fog of revisionism.

Muhammad Ali: His Life and Times is often referred to as the definitive account of the first fifty years of Ali's life. *The Lost Legacy of Muhammad Ali* is the companion volume to that book. It contains all of the essays and articles I've written about Ali over the years. Some of this material has been previously published in article form or as the text for coffee-table photograph books that are now out of print. Other portions of this volume are published here for the first time.

The Lost Legacy of Muhammad Ali is scheduled for publication within a month of four significant anniversaries for Ali. His Olympic triumph (45 years ago), his return from ring exile against Jerry Quarry (35 years), his climactic third fight against Joe Frazier (30 years), and the beating he absorbed at the hands of Larry Holmes (25 years) are significant markers in his ring career. But other athletes have performed with comparable glory in their sport. Ali was special because of what he represented and accomplished apart from boxing.

There is a common thread that runs through this book—the legacy of Muhammad Ali. First, I've made an effort to define Ali's legacy. In the 1960s, he was a symbol of hope for oppressed people everywhere; and he embodied the proposition that, unless there's an irrefutable justification for the killing, war is wrong. Again and again, at great personal risk, he stood up for his principles. And over time, his legacy broadened as he became the embodiment of good will and love.

But Ali's legacy is now imperiled. Ever since he lit the flame at the 1996 Olympics in Atlanta, history has been rewritten to serve political, social, and economic ends. There has been a deliberate distortion of what Ali once believed, said, and stood for. In order to take advantage of his economic potential, it has been deemed desirable to "sanitize" him.

How many young people today know that, for years, Ali embraced a doctrine that preached white people were devils who had been genetically created by an evil scientist named Mr. Yacub. That he proclaimed, "We're not all brothers; you can say we're brothers, but we're not." That in contrast to his present beliefs, he rejected the concepts of a final judgment, an afterlife, and heaven and hell.

Here, a reference to *The Autobiography of Malcolm X* is instructive. That book is a marvelous work about a seminal figure in American life. One reason the book is great is that it's honest. Malcolm doesn't gloss over his early wrongdoing. He writes openly about his criminal past, his hatred toward whites, and the rest of the journey that brought him to the realization that "pilgrims from every land, every color and class and rank, all snore in the same language." It is precisely because Malcolm came from hatred that his words carry extra weight when he says, "In the past, yes, I have made sweeping indictments of all white people. I will never be guilty of that again, as I know now that some white people are truly sincere, that some truly are capable of being brotherly toward a black man. A blanket indictment of all white people is as wrong as when whites make blanket indictments against blacks."

The key is truth. In that regard, the final essay in this book is a story unto itself. It examines the trends that have undermined a full understanding of what Muhammad Ali represented in the 1960s when he was at the peak of his influence. The essay was originally commissioned for inclusion in the remarkable $3,000 silk-and-leather-bound volume, *GOAT*, published by Taschen Books in 2003. Then the image-makers disagreed with its content and the essay was excluded.

I think that's unfortunate. The young Ali was never about image-making. His name was attached to cutting-edge social causes. The greatest service that Ali could perform today would be to use his extraordinary persona to the maximum extent possible to promote tolerance and understanding among all people and, most significantly, between America and the Islamic world. Because of his controversial past, Muhammad is uniquely able to contribute to this cause, which is far more important than selling computers and shoes. But you can't sell products for corporate America and, at the same time, sell hard truths to the world.

Lorraine Hansberry once wrote, "When you start measuring somebody, measure him right. Make sure you done take into account what hills and valleys he come through before he got to wherever he is."

Thus, the thought expressed at the close of the final essay in this book: "Great men are considered great, not only because of what they achieve, but also because of the road they travel to reach their final destination. Sanitizing Muhammad Ali and rounding off the rough edges of his journey is a disservice both to history and to Ali himself. Rather than cultivate historical amnesia, we should cherish the memory of Ali as a warrior and as a gleaming symbol of defiance against an unjust social order when he was young."

Drew "Bundini" Brown and Muhammad Ali.

ESSAYS

Joe Louis and Muhammad Ali.

The Importance of Muhammad Ali

(1996)

Cassius Marcellus Clay, Jr., as Muhammad Ali was once known, was born in Louisville, Kentucky, on January 17, 1942. Louisville was a city with segregated public facilities, noted for the Kentucky Derby, mint juleps, and other reminders of southern aristocracy. Blacks were the servant class in Louisville. They raked manure in the backstretch at Churchill Downs and cleaned other people's homes. Growing up in Louisville, the best on the socio-economic ladder that most black people could realistically hope for was to become a clergyman or a teacher at an all-black public school. In a society where it was often felt that might makes right, "white" was synonymous with both.

Ali's father, Cassius Marcellus Clay, Sr., supported a wife and two sons by painting billboards and signs. Ali's mother, Odessa Grady Clay, worked on occasion as a household domestic. "I remember one time when Cassius was small," Mrs. Clay later recalled. "We were downtown at a five-and-ten-cents store. He wanted a drink of water, and they wouldn't give him one because of his color. And that really affected him. He didn't like that at all, being a child and thirsty. He started crying, and I said, 'Come on, I'll take you someplace and get you some water.' But it really hurt him."

When Cassius Clay was twelve years old, his bike was stolen. That led him to take up boxing under the tutelage of a Louisville policeman named Joe Martin. Clay advanced through the amateur ranks, won a gold medal at the 1960 Olympics in Rome, and turned pro under the guidance of The Louisville Sponsoring Group, a syndicate comprised of eleven wealthy white men.

"Cassius was something in those days," his longtime physician, Ferdie Pacheco, remembers. "He began training in Miami with Angelo Dundee, and Angelo put him in a den of iniquity called the Mary Elizabeth Hotel, because Angelo is one of the most innocent men in the world and it was a cheap hotel. This place was full of pimps, thieves, and drug dealers. And here's Cassius, who comes from a good home, and all of a sudden he's involved with this circus of street people. At first, the hustlers thought he was just another guy to take to the cleaners; another guy to steal from; another guy to sell dope to; another guy to fix up with a girl. He had this incredible innocence about him, and usually that kind of person gets eaten alive in the ghetto. But then the hustlers all fell in love with him, like everybody does, and they started to feel protective of him. If someone tried to sell him a girl, the others would say, 'Leave him alone; he's not into that.' If a guy came around, saying, 'Have a drink,' it was, 'Shut up; he's in training.' But that's the story of Ali's life. He's always been like a little kid, climbing out onto tree limbs, sawing them off behind him, and coming out okay."

In the early stages of his professional career, Cassius Clay was more highly regarded for his charm and personality than for his ring skills. He told the world that he was "The Greatest," but the brutal realities of boxing seemed to dictate otherwise. Then, on February 25, 1964, in one of the most stunning upsets in sports history, Clay knocked out Sonny Liston to become heavyweight champion of the world. Two days later, he shocked the world again by announcing that he had accepted the teachings of a black separatist religion known as the Nation of Islam. And on March 6, 1964, he took the name "Muhammad Ali," which was given to him by his spiritual mentor, Elijah Muhammad.

For the next three years, Ali dominated boxing as thoroughly and magnificently as any fighter ever. But outside the ring, his persona was being sculpted in ways that were even more important. "My first impression of Cassius Clay," author Alex Haley later recalled, "was of someone with an incredibly versatile personality. You never knew quite where he was in psychic posture. He was almost like that shell game, with a pea and three shells. You know; which shell is the pea under? But he had a belief in himself and convictions far stronger than anybody dreamed he would."

As the 1960s grew more tumultuous, Ali became a lightning rod for dissent in America. His message of black pride and black resistance to white domination was on the cutting edge of the era. Not everything he preached was wise, and Ali himself now rejects some of the beliefs that he adhered to then. Indeed, one might find an allegory for his life in a remark he once made to fellow Olympian Ralph Boston. "I played golf," Ali reported. "And I hit the thing long, but I never knew where it was going."

Sometimes, though, Ali knew precisely where he was going. On April 28, 1967, citing his religious beliefs, he refused induction into the United States Army at the height of the war in Vietnam. Ali's refusal followed a blunt statement, voiced fourteen months earlier— "I ain't got no quarrel with them Vietcong." And the American establishment responded with a vengeance, demanding, "Since when did war become a matter of personal quarrels? War is duty. Your country calls; you answer."

On June 20, 1967, Ali was convicted of refusing induction into the United States Armed Forces and sentenced to five years in prison. Four years later, his conviction was unanimously overturned by the United States Supreme Court. But in the interim, he was stripped of his title and precluded from fighting for three-and-a-half years. "He did not believe he would ever fight again," Ali's wife at that time, Belinda Ali, said of her husband's "exile" from boxing. "He wanted to, but he truly believed that he would never fight again."

Meanwhile, Ali's impact was growing—among black Americans; among those who opposed the war in Vietnam; among all people with grievances against The System. "It's hard to imagine that a sports figure could have so much political influence on so many people," observes Julian Bond. And Jerry Izenberg of the *Newark Star-Ledger* recalls the scene in October 1970, when at long last Ali was allowed to return to the ring. "About two days before the fight against Jerry Quarry, it became clear to me that something had changed," Izenberg remembers. "Long lines of people were checking into the hotel. They were dressed differently than the people who used to go to fights. I saw men wearing capes and hats with plumes, and women wearing next-to-nothing at all. Limousines were lined up at the curb. Money was being flashed everywhere. And I was confused, until a friend of mine who was black said to me, 'You don't get it. Don't you understand? This is the heavyweight champion who beat The Man. The Man said he would never fight again, and here he is, fighting in Atlanta, Georgia.'"

Four months later, Ali's comeback was temporarily derailed when he lost to Joe Frazier. It was a fight of truly historic proportions. Nobody in America was neutral that night. "It does me good to lose about once every ten years," Ali jested after the bout. But physically and psychologically, his pain was enormous. Subsequently, Ali avenged his loss to Frazier twice in historic bouts. And ultimately, he won the heavyweight championship of the world an unprecedented three times.

Meanwhile, Ali's religious views were evolving. In the mid-1970s, he began studying the Qur'an more seriously, focusing on Orthodox Islam. His earlier adherence to the teachings of Elijah Muhammad—that white people are "devils" and there is no heaven or hell—was replaced by a spiritual embrace of all people and preparation for his own afterlife. In 1984, Ali spoke out publicly against the separatist doctrine of Louis Farrakhan, declaring, "What he teaches is not at all what we believe in. He represents the time of our struggle in the dark and a time of confusion in us, and we don't want to be associated with that at all." Ali today is a deeply religious man. Although his health is not what it once was, his thought processes remain clear. He is, still, the most recognizable and the most loved person in the world.

But is Muhammad Ali relevant today? In an age when self-dealing and greed have become public policy, does a middle-aged man who suffers from Parkinson's syndrome really matter? At a time when an intrusive worldwide electronic media dominates, and celebrity status and fame are mistaken for heroism, is true heroism possible?

In response to these questions, it should first be noted that, unlike many famous people, Ali is not a creation of the media. He used the media in extraordinary fashion. And certainly, he came along at the right time in terms of television. In 1960, when Cassius Clay won an Olympic gold medal, TV was crawling out of its infancy. The television networks had just learned how to focus cameras on people, build them up, and follow stories through to the end. And Ali loved that. As Jerry Izenberg later observed, "Once Ali found out about television, it was, 'Where? Bring the cameras! I'm ready now.'"

Still, Ali's fame is pure. Athletes today are known as much for their endorsement contracts and salaries as for their competitive performances. Fame now often stems from sports marketing rather than the other way around. Bo Jackson was briefly one of the most famous men in America because of his Nike shoe commercials. Michael Jordan and virtually all of his brethren derive a substantial portion of their visibility from commercial endeavors. Yet, as great an athlete as Michael Jordan is, he doesn't have the ability to move people's hearts and minds the way that Ali has moved them for decades. And what Muhammad Ali means to the world can be viewed from an ever deepening perspective today.

Ali entered the public arena as an athlete. And to many, that's significant. "Sports is a major factor in ideological control," says sociologist Noam Chomsky. "After all, people have minds; they've got to be involved in something; and it's important to make sure they're involved in things that have absolutely no significance. So professional sports is perfect. It instills the right ideas of passivity. It's a way of keeping people diverted from issues like who runs society and who makes the decisions on how their lives are to be led."

But Ali broke the mold. When he appeared on the scene, it was popular among those in the vanguard of the civil rights movement to take the "safe" path. That path wasn't safe for those who participated in the struggle. Martin Luther King, Jr., Medgar Evers, Viola Liuzzo, and other courageous men and women were subjected to economic assaults, violence, and death when they carried the struggle "too far." But the road they traveled was designed to be as non-threatening as possible for white America. White Americans were told, "All that black people want is what you want for your-selves. We're appealing to your conscience."

Then along came Ali, preaching not "white American values," but freedom and equality of a kind rarely seen anywhere in the world. And as if that wasn't threatening enough, Ali attacked the status quo from outside of politics and outside of the accepted strategies of the civil rights movement. "I remember when Ali joined the Nation of Islam," Julian Bond recalls. "The act of joining was not something many of us particularly liked. But the notion he'd do it; that he'd jump out there, join this group that was so despised by mainstream America, and be proud of it, sent a little thrill through you."

"The nature of the controversy," football great Jim Brown, also the founder of the Black Economic Union, said later, "was that white folks could not stand free black folks. White America could not stand to think that a sports hero that it was allowing to make big dollars would embrace something like the Nation of Islam. But this young man had the courage to stand up like no one else and risk, not only his life, but everything else that he had."

Ali himself downplayed his role. "I'm not no leader. I'm a little humble follower," he said in 1964. But to many, he was the ultimate symbol of black pride and black resistance to an unjust social order. Sometimes Ali spoke with humor. "I'm not just saying black is best because I'm black," he told a college audience during his exile from boxing. "I can prove it. If you want some rich dirt, you look for the black dirt. If you want the best bread, you want the whole wheat rye bread. Costs more money, but it's better for your digestive system. You want the best sugar for cooking; it's the brown sugar. The blacker the berry, the sweeter the fruit. If I want a strong cup of coffee, I'll take it black. The coffee gets weak if I integrate it with white cream."

Other times, Ali's remarks were less humorous and more barbed. But for millions of people, the experience of being black changed because of Muhammad Ali. Listen to the voices of some who heard his call:

Bryant Gumbel: One of the reasons the civil rights movement

went forward was that black people were able to overcome their fear. And I honestly believe that, for many black Americans, that came from watching Muhammad Ali. He simply refused to be afraid. And being that way, he gave other people courage.

Alex Haley: We are not white, you know. And it's not an anti-white thing to be proud to be us and to want someone to champion. And Muhammad Ali was the absolute ultimate champion.

Arthur Ashe: Ali didn't just change the image that African-Americans have of themselves. He opened the eyes of a lot of white people to the potential of African-Americans; who we are and what we can be.

Abraham Lincoln once said that he regarded the Emancipation Proclamation as the central act of his administration. "It is a momentous thing," Lincoln wrote, "to be the instrument under Providence of the liberation of a race." Muhammad Ali was such an instrument. As commentator Gil Noble later explained, "Everybody was plugged into this man, because he was taking on America. There had never been anybody in his position who directly addressed himself to racism. Racism was virulent, but you didn't talk about those things. If you wanted to make it in this country, you had to be quiet, carry yourself in a certain way, and not say anything about what was going on, even though there was a knife sticking in your chest. Well, Ali changed all of that. He just laid it out and talked about racism and slavery and all of that stuff. He put it on the table. And everybody who was black, whether they said it overtly or covertly, said 'AMEN.'"

But Ali's appeal would come to extend far beyond black America. When he refused induction into the United States Army, he stood up to armies everywhere in support of the proposition that, "Unless you have a very good reason to kill, war is wrong."

"I don't think Ali was aware of the impact that his not going in the army would have on other people," says his longtime friend,

Howard Bingham. "Ali was just doing what he thought was right for him. He had no idea at the time that this was going to effect how people all over the United States would react to the war and the draft."

Many Americans vehemently condemned Ali's stand. It came at a time when most people in the United States still supported the war. But as Julian Bond later observed, "When Ali refused to take the symbolic step forward, everybody knew about it moments later. You could hear people talking about it on street corners. It was on everyone's lips."

"The government didn't need Ali to fight the war," Ramsey Clark, then the Attorney General of the United States, recalls. "But they would have loved to put him in the service; get his picture in there; maybe give him a couple of stripes on his sleeve, and take him all over the world. Think of the power that would have had in Africa, Asia, and South America. Here's this proud American serviceman, fighting symbolically for his country. They would have loved to do that."

But instead, what the government got was a reaffirmation of Ali's earlier statement—"I ain't got no quarrel with them Vietcong." "And that rang serious alarm bells," says Noam Chomsky, "because it raised the question of why poor people in the United States were being forced by rich people in the United States to kill poor people in Vietnam. Putting it simply, that's what it amounted to. And Ali put it very simply in ways that people could understand."

Ali's refusal to accept induction placed him once and for all at the vortex of the 1960s. "You had riots in the streets; you had assassinations; you had the war in Vietnam," Dave Kindred of the *Atlanta Constitution* remembers. "It was a violent, turbulent, almost indecipherable time in America, and Ali was in all of those fires at once, in addition to being heavyweight champion of the world."

That championship was soon taken from Ali, but he never wavered from his cause. Speaking to a college audience, he proclaimed, "I would like to say to those of you who think I've lost so much, I have gained everything. I have peace of heart; I have a clear free conscience. And I'm proud. I wake up happy. I go to bed happy. And if I go to jail, I'll go to jail happy. Boys go to war and die for what they believe, so I don't see why the world is so shook up over me suffering for what I believe. What's so unusual about that?"

"It really impressed me that Ali gave up his title," says former heavyweight champion Larry Holmes, who understands Ali's sacrifice as well as anyone. "Once you have it, you never want to lose it; because once you lose it, it's hard to get it back."

But by the late 1960s, Ali was more than heavyweight champion. That had become almost a side issue. He was a living embodiment of the proposition that principles matter. And the most powerful thing about him was no longer his fists; it was his conscience and the composure with which he carried himself:

Kwame Toure [formerly known as Stokely Carmichael]: Muhammad Ali used himself as a perfect instrument to advance the struggle of humanity by demonstrating clearly that principles are more important than material wealth. It's not just what Ali did. The way he did it was just as important.

Wilbert McClure [Ali's roommate and fellow gold-medal winner at the 1960 Olympics]: He always carried himself with his head high and with grace and composure. And we can't say that about all of his detractors; some of them in political office, some of them in pulpits, some of them thought of as nice upstanding citizens. No, we can't say that about all of them.

Charles Morgan [former Director of the ACLU Southern Office]: I remember thinking at the time, what kind of a foolish world am I living in where people want to put this man in jail.

Dave Kindred: He was one thing, always. He was always brave.

Ali was far from perfect, and it would do him a disservice not to acknowledge his flaws. It's hard to imagine a person so powerful yet at times so naive; almost on the order of Forrest Gump. On occasion, Ali has acted irrationally. He cherishes honor and is an honorable person, but too often excuses dishonorable behavior in others. His accommodation with dictators like Mobuto Sese Seko and Ferdinand Marcos and his willingness to fight in their countries stood in stark contrast to his love of freedom. There is nothing redeeming in one black person calling another black person a "gorilla," which was the label that Ali affixed to Joe Frazier. Nor should one gloss over Ali's past belief in racial separatism and the profligate womanizing of his younger days. But the things that Ali has done right in his life far outweigh the mistakes of his past. And the rough edges of his earlier years have been long since been forgiven or forgotten.

What remains is a legacy of monumental proportions and a living reminder of what people can be. Muhammad Ali's influence on an entire nation, black and white, and a whole world of nations has been incalculable. He's not just a champion. A champion is someone who wins an athletic competition. Ali goes beyond that.

It was inevitable that someone would come along and do what Jackie Robinson did. Robinson did it in a glorious way that personified his own dignity and courage. But if Jackie Robinson hadn't been there, someone else—Roy Campanella, Willie Mays, Henry Aaron—would have stepped in with his own brand of excitement and grace and opened baseball's doors. With or without Jack Johnson, eventually a black man would have won the heavyweight championship of the world. And sooner or later, there would have been a black athlete who, like Joe Louis, was universally admired and loved. But Ali carved out a place in history that was, and remains, uniquely his own. And it's unlikely that anyone other than Muhammad Ali could have created and fulfilled that role. Ali didn't just mirror his times. He wasn't a passive figure carried along by currents stronger than he was. He fought the current; he swam against the tide. He stood for something, stayed with it, and prevailed.

Muhammad Ali is an international treasure. More than anyone else of his generation, he belongs to the people of the world and is loved by them. No matter what happens in the years ahead, he has already made us better. He encouraged millions of people to believe in themselves, raise their aspirations, and accomplish things that might not have been done without him. He wasn't just a standard-bearer for black Americans. He stood up for everyone.

And that's the importance of Muhammad Ali.

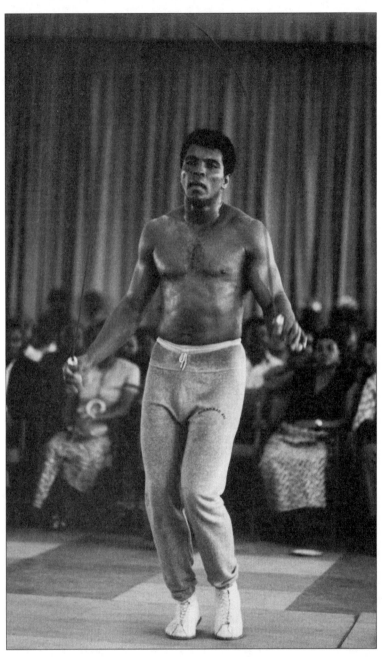

Training in 1974.

Muhammad Ali
and Boxing
(1996)

"You could spend twenty years studying Ali," Dave Kindred once wrote, "and still not know what he is or who he is. He's a wise man, and he's a child. I've never seen anyone who was so giving and, at the same time, so self-centered. He's either the most complex guy that I've ever been around or the most simple. And I still can't figure out which it is. I mean, I truly don't know. We were sure who Ali was only when he danced before us in the dazzle of the ring lights. Then he could hide nothing."

And so it was that the world first came to know Muhammad Ali, not as a person; not as a social, political, or religious figure; but as a fighter. His early professional bouts infuriated and entertained as much as they impressed. Cassius Clay held his hands too low. He backed away from punches, rather than bobbing and weaving out of danger, and lacked true knockout power. Purists cringed when he predicted the round in which he intended to knock out his opponent, and grimaced when he did so and bragged about each new conquest.

Then, at age 22, Clay challenged Sonny Liston for the world heavyweight crown. Liston was widely regarded as the most intimidating, ferocious, powerful fighter of his era. Clay was such a prohibitive underdog that Robert Lipsyte, who covered the bout for *The New York Times*, was instructed to "find out the directions from the arena to the nearest hospital, so I wouldn't waste deadline time getting there after Clay was knocked out." But as David Ben-Gurion once proclaimed, "Anyone who doesn't believe in miracles is not a realist." Cassius Clay knocked out Sonny Liston to become heavyweight champion of the world.

Officially, Ali's reign as champion was divided into three segments. And while he fought through the administrations of seven Presidents, his greatness as a fighter was most clearly on display in the three years after he first won the crown. During the course of thirty-seven months, Ali fought ten times. No heavyweight in history has defended his title more frequently against more formidable opposition in more dominant fashion than Ali did in those years.

Boxing, in the first instance, is about not getting hit. "And I can't be hit," Ali told the world. "It's impossible for me to lose, because there's not a man on earth with the speed and ability to beat me." In his rematch with Liston, which ended in a first-round knockout, Ali was hit only twice. Victories over Floyd Patterson, George Chuvalo, Henry Cooper, Brian London, and Karl Mildenberger followed. Then, on November 14, 1966, Ali did battle against Cleveland Williams. Over the course of three rounds, Ali landed more than one hundred punches, scored four knockdowns, and was hit a total of three times. "The hypocrites and phonies are all shook up because everything I said would come true did come true," Ali chortled afterward. "I said I was The Greatest, and they thought I was just acting the fool. Now, instead of admitting that I'm the best heavyweight in all history, they don't know what to do."

Ali's triumph over Cleveland Williams was followed by victories over Ernie Terrell and Zora Folley. Then, after refusing induction into the United States Army, he was stripped of his title and forced out of boxing. "If I never fight again, this is the last of the champions," Ali said of his, and boxing's, plight. "The next title is a political belt, a racial belt, an organization belt. There's no more real world champion until I'm physically beat."

In October 1970, Ali was allowed to return to boxing, but his skills were no longer the same. The legs that had allowed him to "dance" for fifteen rounds without stopping no longer carried him as surely around the ring. His reflexes, while still superb, were no longer lightning fast. Ali prevailed in his first two comeback fights, against Jerry Quarry and Oscar Bonavena. Then he challenged Joe Frazier, who was the "organization" champion by virtue of victories over Buster Mathis and Jimmy Ellis.

"Champion of the world? Ain't but one champion," Ali said before his first bout against Frazier. "How you gonna have two champions of the world? He's an alternate champion. The real champion is back now." But Frazier thought otherwise. And on March 8, 1971, he bested Ali over fifteen brutal rounds. "He's not a great boxer," Ali said afterward. "But he's a great slugger, a great street fighter, a bull fighter. He takes a lot of punches, his eyes close, and he just keeps coming. I figured he could take the punches. But one thing surprised me in this fight, and that's that he landed his left hook as regular as he did. Usually, I don't get hit over and over with the same punch, and he hit me solid a lot of times."

Some fighters can't handle defeat. They fly so high when they're on top, that a loss brings them irrevocably crashing down. "What was interesting to me after the loss to Frazier," says Ferdie Pacheco, "was we'd seen this undefeatable guy; now how was he going to handle defeat? Was he going to be a cry-baby? Was he going to be crushed? Well, what we found out was, this guy takes defeat like he takes victory. All he said was, I'll beat him next time."

What Ali said was plain and simple: "I got to whup Joe Frazier, because he beat me. Anybody would like to say, 'I retired undefeated.' I can't say that no more. But if I could say, 'I got beat, but I came back and beat him,' I'd feel better."

Following his loss to Frazier, Ali won ten fights in a row; eight of them against world-class opponents. Then, in March 1973, he stumbled, when a little-known fighter named Ken Norton broke his jaw in the second round en route to a twelve-round upset decision. "I knew something was strange," Ali said after the bout, "because, if a bone is broken, the whole internalness in your body, everything, is nauseating. I didn't know what it was, but I could feel my teeth moving around, and I had to hold my teeth extra tight to keep the bottom from moving. My trainers wanted me to stop. But I was thinking about those nineteen thousand people in the arena; and *Wide World of Sports*, millions of people at home watching in sixty-two countries. So what I had to do was put up a good fight; go the distance, and not get hit on the jaw again.'"

Now Ali had a new target; a priority ahead of even Joe Frazier. "After Ali got his jaw broke, he wanted Norton bad," recalls Lloyd Wells, a longtime Ali confidante. "Herbert Muhammad [Ali's manager] was trying to put him in another fight, and Ali kept saying, 'No, get me Norton. I want Norton.' Herbert was saying, but we got a big purse; we got this, and we got that. And Ali was saying, 'No, just get me Norton. I don't want nobody but Norton.'"

Ali got Norton—and beat him. Then, after an interim bout against Rudi Lubbers, he got Joe Frazier again—and beat him too. From a technical point of view, the second Ali-Frazier bout was probably Ali's best performance after his exile from boxing. He did what he wanted to do, showing flashes of what he'd once been as a fighter but never would be again. Then Ali journeyed to Zaire to challenge George Foreman, who had dethroned Frazier to become heavyweight champion of the world.

"Foreman can punch but he can't fight," Ali said of his next foe. But most observers thought that Foreman could do both. As was the case when Ali fought Sonny Liston, he entered the ring a heavy underdog. Still, studying his opponent's armor, Ali thought he detected a flaw. Foreman's punching power was awesome, but his stamina and will were suspect. Thus, the "rope-a-dope" was born.

"The strategy on Ali's part was to cover up, because George was like a tornado," former boxing great Archie Moore, who was one of Foreman's cornermen that night, recalls. "And when you see a tornado coming, you run into the house and you cover up. You go into the basement and get out of the way of that strong wind, because you know that otherwise it's going to blow you away. That's what Ali did. He covered up and the storm was raging, but after a while, the storm blew itself out."

Or phrased differently, "Yeah, Ali let Foreman punch himself out," says Jerry Izenberg. "But the rope-a-dope wouldn't have worked against Foreman for anyone in the world except Ali, because on top of everything else, Ali was tougher than everyone else. No one in the world except Ali could have taken George Foreman's punches."

Ali stopped Foreman in the eighth round to regain the heavy-weight championship. Then, over the next thirty months at the peak of his popularity as champion, he fought nine times. Those bouts showed Ali to be a courageous fighter, but a fighter on the decline. Like most aging combatants, he did his best to put a positive spin on things. But viewed in realistic terms, "I'm more experienced" translated into "I'm getting older." "I'm stronger at this weight" meant "I should lose a few pounds." And "I'm more patient now" was a cover for "I'm slower." Eight of Ali's first nine fights during his second reign as champion did little to enhance his legacy. But sandwiched in between matches against the likes of Jean-Pierre Coopman and Richard Dunn and mediocre showings against more legitimate adversaries, Ali won what might have been the greatest fight of all time.

On October 1, 1975, Ali and Joe Frazier met in the Philippines, six miles outside of Manila, to do battle for the third time.

"You have to understand the premise behind that fight," Ferdie Pacheco recalls. "The first fight was life and death, and Frazier won. Second fight, Ali figures him out; no problem, relatively easy victory for Ali. Then Ali beats Foreman, and Frazier's sun sets. And I don't care what anyone says now; all of us thought that Joe Frazier was shot. We all thought that this was going to be an easy fight. Ali comes out, dances around, and knocks him out in eight or nine rounds. That's what we figured. And you know what happened in that fight. Ali took a beating like you'd never believe anyone could take. When he said afterward that it was the closest thing he'd ever known to death—let me tell you something; if dying is that hard, I'd hate to see it coming. But Frazier took the same beating. And in the fourteenth round, Ali just about took his head off. I was cringing. The heat was awesome; both men were dehydrated; the place was like a time-bomb. I thought we were close to a fatality. It was a terrible moment, and then Joe Frazier's corner stopped it."

"Ali-Frazier III was Ali-Frazier III," says Jerry Izenberg. "There's nothing to compare it with. I've never witnessed anything like it. And I'll tell you something else. Both fighters won that night, and both fighters lost."

Boxing is a tough business. The nature of the game is that fighters get hit. Ali himself inflicted a lot of damage on ring opponents during the course of his career. And in return: "I've been hit a lot," he acknowledged, one month before the third Frazier fight. "I take punishment every day in training. I take punishment in my fights. I take a lot of punishment; I just don't show it."

Still, as Ferdie Pacheco notes, "The human brain wasn't meant to get hit by a heavyweight punch. And the older you get, the more susceptible you are to damage. When are you best? Between fifteen and thirty. At that age, you're growing, you're strong, you're developing. You can take punches and come back. But inevitably, if you keep fighting, you reach an age when every punch can cause damage. Nature begins giving you little bills and the amount keeps escalating, like when you owe money to the IRS and the government keeps adding and compounding the damage."

In Manila, Joe Frazier landed 440 punches, many of those to Ali's head. After Manila would have been a good time for Ali to stop boxing, but too many people had a vested interest in his continuing to fight. Harold Conrad served for years as a publicist for Ali's bouts. "You get a valuable piece of property like Ali," Conrad said shortly before his death. "How are you going to put it out of business? It's like shutting down a factory or closing down a big successful corporation. The people who are making money off the workers just don't want to do it."

Thus, Ali fought on. In 1977, he was hurt badly but came back to win a close decision over Earnie Shavers. "In the second round, I had him in trouble," Shavers remembers. "I threw a right hand over Ali's jab, and I hurt him. He kind of wobbled. But Ali was so cunning, I didn't know if he was hurt or playing fox. I found out later that he was hurt; but he waved me in, so I took my time to be careful. I didn't want to go for the kill and get killed. And Ali was the kind of guy who, when you thought you had him hurt, he always seemed to come back. The guy seemed to pull off a miracle each time. I hit him a couple of good shots, but he recovered better than any other fighter I've known."

Next up for Ali was Leon Spinks, a novice with an Olympic gold medal but only seven professional fights.

"Spinks was in awe of Ali," Ron Borges of the *Boston Globe* recalls. "The day before their first fight, I was having lunch in the coffee shop at Caesar's Palace with Leon and [his trainer] Sam Solomon.

No one knew who Leon was. Then Ali walked in, and everyone went crazy. 'Look, there's Ali! Omigod, it's him!' And Leon was like everybody else. He got all excited. He was shouting, 'Look, there he is! There's Ali!' In twenty-four hours, they'd be fighting each other, but right then, Leon was ready to carry Ali around the room on his shoulders."

The next night, Spinks captured Ali's title with a relentless fifteen-round assault. Seven months later, Ali returned the favor, regaining the championship with a fifteen round victory of his own. Then he retired from boxing, but two years later made an ill-advised comeback against Larry Holmes.

"Before the Holmes fight, you could clearly see the beginnings of Ali's physical deterioration," remembers Barry Frank, who was representing Ali in various commercial endeavors on behalf of IMG. "The huskiness had already come into his voice, and he had a little bit of a balance problem. Sometimes he'd get up off a chair and, not stagger, but maybe take a half step to get his balance."

Realistically speaking, it was obvious that Ali had no chance of beating Larry Holmes. But there was always that kernel of doubt. Would beating Holmes be any more extraordinary than knocking out Sonny Liston and George Foreman? Ali himself fanned the flames. "I'm so happy going into this fight," he said shortly before the bout. "I'm dedicating this fight to all the people who've been told, you can't do it. People who drop out of school because they're told they're dumb. People who go to crime because they don't think they can find jobs. I'm dedicating this fight to all of you people who have a Larry Holmes in your life. I'm gonna whup my Holmes, and I want you to whup your Holmes."

But Holmes put it more succinctly. "Ali is thirty-eight years old. His mind is making a date that his body can't keep."

Holmes was right. It was a horrible night. Old and seriously debilitated from the effects of an improperly prescribed drug called Thyrolar, Ali was a shell of his former self. He had no reflexes, no legs, no punch. Nothing, except his pride and the crowd chanting, "Ali! Ali!"

"I really thought something bad might happen that night," Jerry Izenberg recalls. "And I was praying that it wouldn't be the something that we dread most in boxing. I've been at three fights where fighters died, and it sort of found a home in the back of my mind. I was saying, I don't want this man to get hurt. Whoever won the fight was irrelevant to me."

It wasn't an athletic contest; just a brutal beating that went on and on. Later, some observers claimed that Holmes lay back because of his fondness for Ali. But Holmes was being cautious, not compassionate. "I love the man," he later acknowledged. "But when the bell rung, I didn't even know his name."

"By the ninth round, Ali had stopped fighting altogether," Lloyd Wells remembers. "He was just defending himself, and not doing a good job of that. Then, in the ninth round, Holmes hit him with a punch to the body, and Ali screamed. I never will forget that as long as I live. Ali screamed."

The fight was stopped after eleven rounds. An era in boxing— and an entire historical era—was over. And now, years later, in addition to his more important social significance, Ali is widely recognized as the greatest fighter of all time. He was graced with almost unearthly physical skills, and did everything that his body allowed him to do. In a sport that is often brutal and violent, he cast a long and graceful shadow.

How good was Ali?

"In the early days," Ferdie Pacheco recalls, "he fought as though he had a glass jaw and was afraid to get hit. He had the hyper reflexes of a frightened man. He was so fast that you had the feeling, 'This guy is scared to death; he can't be that fast normally.' Well, he wasn't scared. He was fast beyond belief and smart. Then he went into exile; and when he came back, he couldn't move like lightning anymore. Everyone wondered, 'What happens now when he gets hit?' That's when we learned something else about him. That sissy-looking, soft-looking, beautiful-looking, child-man was one of the toughest guys who ever lived."

Ali didn't have one-punch knockout power. His most potent offensive weapon was speed; the speed of his jab and straight right hand. But when he sat down on his punches, as he did against Joe Frazier in Manila, he hit harder than most heavyweights. And in addition to his other assets, he had superb footwork, the ability to take a punch, and all of the intangibles that go into making a great fighter.

"Ali fought all wrong," acknowledges Jerry Izenberg. "Boxing people would say to me, 'Any guy who can do this will beat him. Any guy who can do that will beat him.' And after a while, I started saying back to them, 'So you're telling me that any guy who can outjab the fastest jabber in the world can beat him. Any guy who can slip that jab, which is like lightning, not get hit with a hook off the jab, get inside, and pound on his ribs can beat him. Any guy. Well, you're asking for the greatest fighter who ever lived, so this kid must be pretty good.'"

And on top of everything else, the world never saw Muhammad Ali at his peak as a fighter. When Ali was forced into exile in 1967, he was getting better with virtually every fight. The Ali who fought Cleveland Williams, Ernie Terrell, and Zora Folley was bigger, stronger, more confident, and more skilled than the 22-year-old who, three years earlier, had defeated Sonny Liston. But when Ali returned, his ring skills were diminished. He was markedly slower, and his legs weren't the same.

"I was better when I was young," Ali acknowledged later. "I was more experienced when I was older. I was stronger; I had more belief in myself. Except for Sonny Liston, the men I fought when I was young weren't near the fighters that Joe Frazier and George Foreman were. But I had my speed when I was young. I was faster on my legs, and my hands were faster."

Thus, the world never saw what might have been. What it did see, though, in the second half of Ali's career, was an incredibly courageous fighter. Not only did Ali fight his heart out in the ring; he fought the most dangerous foes imaginable. Many champions avoid facing tough challengers. When Joe Louis was champion, he refused to fight certain black contenders. After Joe Frazier defeated Ali, his next defenses were against Terry Daniels and Ron Stander. Once George Foreman won the title, his next bout was against Jose Roman. But Ali had a different creed. "I fought the best, because if you want to be a true champion, you got to show people that you can whup everybody," he proclaimed.

"I don't think there's a fighter in his right mind that wouldn't admire Ali," says Earnie Shavers. "We all dreamed about being just half the fighter that Ali was." And of course, each time Ali entered the ring, the pressure on him was palpable. "It's not like making a movie where, if you mess up, you stop and reshoot," he said shortly before Ali-Frazier III. "When that bell rings and you're out there, the whole world is watching and it's real."

But Ali was more than a great fighter. He was the standard-bearer for boxing's modern era. The 1960s promised athletes who were bigger and faster than their predecessors, and Ali was the prototype for that mold. Also, he was part and parcel of the changing economics of boxing. Ali arrived just in time for the advent of satellites and closed circuit television. He carried heavyweight championship boxing beyond the confines of the United States, and popularized the sport around the globe.

Almost always, the public sees boxers as warriors without ever realizing their soft human side. But the whole world saw Ali's humanity. "I was never a boxing fan until Ali came along," is a refrain one frequently hears. And while "the validity of boxing is always hanging by a thread," England's Hugh McIlvanney, who coined that phrase, acknowledges, "Ali was boxing's salvation."

An Ali fight was always an event. Ali put that in perspective when he said, "I truly believe I'm fighting for the betterment of people. I'm not fighting for diamonds or Rolls-Royces or mansions, but to help mankind. Before a fight, I get myself psyched up. It gives me more power, knowing there's so much involved and so many people are gonna be helped by my victory." To which Gil Noble adds, "When Ali got in the ring, there was a lot more at stake than the title. When that man got in the ring, he took all of us with him."

Also, for virtually his entire career, being around Ali was fun. Commenting on young Cassius Clay, Don Elbaum remembers, "I was the matchmaker for a show in Pittsburgh when he fought Charlie Powell. We were staying at a place called Carlton House. And two or three days before the fight, Cassius, which was his name then, decided to visit a black area of Pittsburgh. It was winter, real cold. But he went out, walking the streets, just talking to people. And I've never seen anything like it in my life. When he came back to the hotel around six o'clock, there were three hundred people following him. The Pied Piper couldn't have done any better. And the night of the fight, the weather was awful. There was a blizzard; the schools were shut down. Snow kept falling; it was windy. Conditions were absolutely horrible. And the fight sold out."

Some athletes are engaging when they're young, but lose their charm as their celebrity status grows. But Michael Katz of the *New York Daily News* recalls the day when Ali, at the peak of his popularity, defended his title against Richard Dunn. "On the day of the fight," Katz remembers, "Ali got bored so he decided to hold a press conference. Word got around; Ali came downstairs, and we went to a conference room in the hotel but it wasn't set up yet. So every member of the press followed him around. We were like mice, going from room to room, until finally the hotel management set us up someplace. And Ali proceeded to have us all in stitches. He imitated every opponent he'd ever fought, including Richard Dunn, who he hadn't fought yet. And he was marvelous. You'd have paid more money to see Muhammad Ali on stage at that point than you'd pay today for Robin Williams."

And Ali retained his charm when he got old. "The first Ali fight I ever covered," says Ron Borges, "was the one against Leon Spinks, where Ali said it made him look silly to talk up an opponent with only seven professional fights so he wasn't talking. And I said to myself, 'Great. Here I am, a young reporter about to cover the most verbally gifted athlete in history, and the man's not talking.' Anyway, I was at one of Ali's workouts. Ali finished sparring, picked up a microphone, and told us all what he'd said before: 'I'm not talking.' And then he went on for about ninety minutes. Typical Ali; the funniest monologue I've ever heard. And when he was done, he put the microphone down, smiled that incredible smile, and told us all, 'But I'm not talking.' I'll always remember the joy of being around Ali," Borges says in closing. "It was fun. And covering the heavyweights isn't much fun anymore. Ali took that with him when he left, and things have been pretty ugly lately."

Muhammad Ali did too much for boxing. And the sport isn't the same without him.

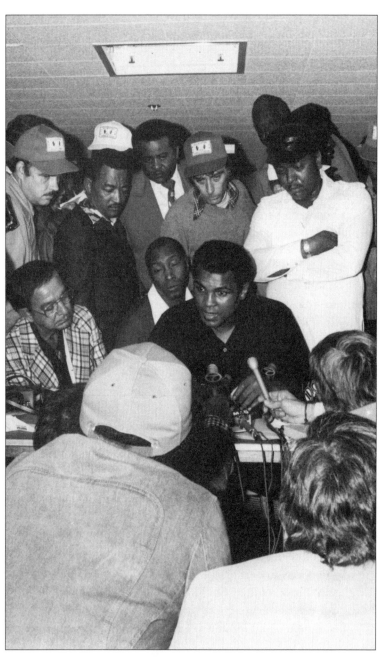

Addressing the media.

Muhammad Ali and Congress Remembered
(2000)

At long last, Congress has enacted the Muhammad Ali Boxing Reform Act. As a cure for what ails boxing, the proposed legislation leaves a lot to be desired. Still, it's a step in the right direction. Meanwhile, Senator Jim Bunning of Kentucky is sponsoring legislation that would authorize President Clinton to award Ali with a Congressional Gold Medal (the highest civilian honor that Congress can bestow upon an individual). Thus, it's worth remembering what an earlier generation of Congressmen had to say about Muhammad Ali at the height of the war in Vietnam.

On February 17, 1966, Ali was reclassified 1-A by his draft board and uttered the immortal words, "I ain't got no quarrel with them Vietcong." One month later, Congressman Frank Clark of Pennsylvania rose in Congress and called upon the American public to boycott Ali's upcoming bout against George Chuvalo:

> The heavyweight champion of the world turns my stomach. I am not a superpatriot. But I feel that each man, if he really is a man, owes to his country a willingness to protect it and serve it in time of need. From this standpoint, the heavyweight champion has been a complete and total disgrace. I urge the citizens of the nation as a whole to boycott any of his performances. To leave these theater seats empty would be the finest tribute possible to that boy whose hearse may pass by the open

doors of the theater on Main Street USA.

In 1967, Ali refused induction into the United States Army, at which point he was stripped of his title and denied a license to box in all fifty states. That same year, he was indicted, tried, convicted, and sentenced to five years in prison. Then, in October 1969, while the appeal of his conviction was pending, ABC announced plans to have Ali serve as a TV-commentator for an upcoming amateur boxing competition between the United States and Soviet Union. Congressman Fletcher Thompson of Georgia objected:

> I take the floor today to protest the network that has announced it will use Cassius Clay as a commentator for these contests. I consider this an affront to loyal Americans everywhere, although it will obviously receive much applause in some of the hippie circles. Maybe the American Broadcasting System feels that it needs to appeal more to the hippies and yippies of America than to loyal Americans.

In December 1969, there were reports that Governor Claude Kirk of Florida would grant Ali a license to fight Joe Frazier in Tampa. Congressman Robert Michel of Illinois took to the podium of the United States House of Representatives to protest:

> Clay has been stripped of his heavyweight title for dodging the draft. And I consider it an insult to patriotic Americans everywhere to permit his reentry into the respected ranks of boxing. It should be recalled that Mr. Clay gave as one of his excuses for not wanting to be drafted that he is in reality a minister and that even boxing is antagonistic to his religion. But apparently, he is willing to fight anyone but the Vietcong.

Ultimately, the authorities in Florida refused to give Ali a license to box. Then, in September 1970, it was announced that Ali would fight Jerry Quarry in Georgia. Once again, Congressman Michel had his say:

I read with disgust today the article in the *Washington Post* concerning the upcoming fight of this country's most famous draft dodger, Cassius Clay. The article said that Mr. Clay was out of shape, overweight, and winded. No doubt, this comes from his desperate and concerted efforts to stay out of the military service while thousands of patriotic young men are fighting and dying in Vietnam. Apparently, Mr. Clay feels himself entitled to the full protection of the law, yet does not feel he has to sacrifice anything to preserve the institutions that protect him. Cassius Clay cannot hold a candle to the average American boy who is willing to defend his country in perilous times.

Ali fought Jerry Quarry in Atlanta on October 26, 1970. Then a federal district court decision paved the way for him to fight Oscar Bonavena on December 7th (the anniversary of Pearl Harbor) in New York. After that, he signed to fight Joe Frazier at Madison Square Garden. Each fighter was to receive the previously unheard-of sum of $2,500,000. That outraged Congressman John Rarick of Louisiana, who spoke to his colleagues as follows:

Veterans who have fought our nation's wars feel that any man unwilling to fight for his country is unworthy of making a profit or receiving public acclaim in it. Cassius Clay is a convicted draft dodger sentenced to a five-year prison term which he is not serving. What right has he to claim the privilege of appearing in a boxing match to be nationally televised? The Clay affair approaches a crisis in national indignation.

On March 8, 1971, Ali lost a hard-fought fifteen-round decision to Joe Frazier. Meanwhile, he remained free on bail while the United States Supreme Court considered the appeal of his criminal conviction. This was too much for Congressman George Andrews of Alabama, who spoke to his brethren and compared Ali to Lieutenant William Calley, who had been convicted of murder in the massacre of 22 South Vietnamese civilians at Mylai:

Last night, I was sickened and sad when I heard about that poor little fellow who went down to Fort Benning. He had barely graduated from high school. He volunteered and offered his life for his country. He was taught to kill. He was sent to Vietnam. And he wound up back at Fort Benning, where he was indicted and convicted for murder in the first degree for carrying out orders. I also thought about another young man about his age; one Cassius Clay, alias Muhammad Ali, who several years ago defied the United States government, thumbed his nose at the flag, and is still walking the streets making millions of dollars fighting for pay, not for his country. That is an unequal distribution of justice.

On June 28, 1971, fifty months to the day after Ali had refused induction, the United States Supreme Court unanimously reversed his conviction, and all criminal charges pending against him were dismissed. The next day, Congressman William Nichols of Alabama expressed his outrage:

The United States Supreme Court has given another black eye to the United States Armed Forces. The decision overturning the draft evasion conviction of Cassius Clay is a stinging rebuke to the 240,000 Americans still serving in Vietnam and the 50,000 Americans who lost their lives there. I wish the members of the Supreme Court would assist me when I try to explain to a father why his son must serve in Vietnam or when I attempt to console a widow or the parents of a young man who has died in a war that Cassius Clay was exempted from.

Not to be outdone, Congressman Joe Waggonner of Louisiana echoed his fellow lawmaker's expression of contempt:

The United States Supreme Court has issued the edict that Cassius Clay does not have to be inducted because he does not believe in war. No draft-age young man believes in a war that he will have to fight, nor does any parent of a draft-age son believe in a war that their own flesh and blood will have to fight and possibly give his life in so doing. But our people have always heeded the call of their country when asked, not because they love war, but because their country has asked them to do so. And I feel strongly about this. If Cassius Clay does not have to be drafted because of questionable religious beliefs or punished for refusing induction simply because he is black or because he is a prizefighter—and I can see no other real justification for the Court's action—then all other young men who wish it should also be allowed a draft exemption. Cassius Clay is a phony. He knows it, the Supreme Court knows it, and everyone else knows it.

Times change.

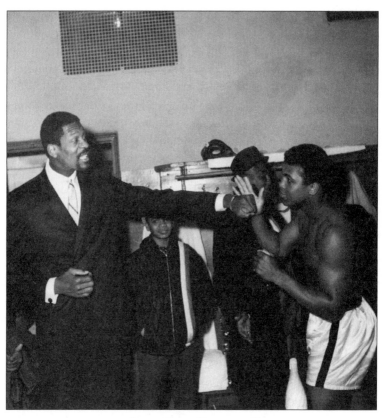

Ali with Bill Russell.

The Athlete of
the Century
(1999)

As 1999 moves toward its long-awaited close, there have been numerous attempts to designate "The Athlete of the Century." Whoever is accorded the honor will doubtless also be recognized as "Athlete of the Millennium." The consensus list for number one has boiled down to three finalists—Babe Ruth, Muhammad Ali and Michael Jordan. There's no right or wrong answer, just points of view.

It's hard to imagine anyone being better in a sport than Michael Jordan was in basketball. His exploits are still fresh in the mind, so suffice it to say that the Chicago Bulls won six world championships during his reign and Jordan was named the series' Most Valuable Player on all six occasions. He led the NBA in scoring ten times, has the highest career scoring average in league history, and was one of the best defensive players ever.

Babe Ruth had an unparalleled genius for the peculiarities of baseball. In 1919, the American League record for home runs in a season was twelve. Ruth hit 29 homers that year, and 54 the year after. In 1927, the year Ruth hit 60 home runs, no other other *team* in the American League had as many. Indeed, in all of major league baseball, there were only 922 home runs hit that year. In other words, Babe Ruth hit 6.5% of all the home runs hit in the entire season.

Ruth's lifetime batting average was .342. Two-thirds of a century

Babe Ruth

after his career ended, he stands second in RBIs, second in runs scored, and second in home runs. And these marks were established despite the fact that Ruth was a pitcher during the first five years of his career. In 1916, at age 21, he pitched nine shutouts en route to a 23 and 12 record and led the league with an earned run average of 1.75. From 1915 through 1919, he won 94 games, lost only 46, and compiled an earned-run average of 2.28. In other words, if Mark McGwire pitched 29-2/3 consecutive scoreless innings in the World Series (which Ruth once did; a record that stood for 43 years), you'd have a phenomenon approaching The Babe. And one thing more. Ruth was a winner. He was with the Boston Red Sox for five full seasons, and they won the World Series in three of them. Then he was traded to the Yankees, who had never won a World Series, and the Yankee dynasty began.

As for Ali, a strong argument can be made that he was the greatest fighter of all time. His lifetime record of 56 wins and 5 losses has been matched by others. But no heavyweight ever had the inquisitors that Ali had—George Foreman, Sonny Liston twice, and Joe Frazier three times. Ali in his prime was the most beautiful fighting machine ever assembled. Pound-for-pound, Sugar Ray Robinson might have been better. But that's like saying, if Jerry West had been six-foot-six, he would have been just as good as Jordan. You are what you are.

Ali fought the way Michael Jordan played basketball. Michael

Jordan played basketball the way Ali fought. Unfortunately, Jordan didn't play baseball the way Ruth did. But then again, I doubt that Ruth would have been much of a basketball player. However, The Babe was known to punch out people rather effectively as a young man.

Thus, looking at Michael Jordan, Babe Ruth, and Muhammad Ali from a purely athletic point of view, it's Jordan (three points for first place), Ruth (two points for second place), and Ali (one point for third place) in that order.

Michael Jordan

But is pure athletic ability the standard? If pure athleticism is the only test, men like Jim Thorpe, Jim Brown and Carl Lewis should also be finalists in the competition for "Athlete of the Century." The fact that they aren't stands testament to the view that something more than achievement on the playing field must be measured; that social impact is also relevant. That's a bit like saying maybe Ronald Reagan should be considered the greatest actor of the twentieth century because of his impact on society. But here goes.

Ruth, Ali and Jordan reflected the eras in which they were at their respective athletic peaks. Ruth personified "The Roaring Twenties." Ali was at the heart of the social and political turmoil of the 1960s. And Michael Jordan speaks to "The Nineties" with its booming stock market, heightened commercialism, and athletes as computer-action-game heroes.

Jordan hasn't changed society. Not yet, anyway. Babe Ruth

brought sports into the mainstream of American culture and earned adulation unmatched in his time. Nor was The Babe's impact confined to the United States. During World War II, long after his playing days were over, Japanese soldiers sought to insult their American counterparts by shouting "to hell with Babe Ruth" at Guadalcanal. Meanwhile, Ali (to use one of his favorite phrases) "shook up the world" and served as an inspiration and beacon of hope, not just in the United States, but for oppressed people around the globe.

One can argue that Jack Johnson, Joe Louis, and Jackie Robinson all had a greater societal impact than Ali. Arthur Ashe once opined, "Within the United States, Jack Johnson had a larger impact than Ali because he was the first. Nothing that any African-American had done up until that time had the same impact as Jack Johnson's fight against James Jeffries."

Joe Louis' hold on the American psyche was so great that the last words spoken by a young man choking to death in the gas chamber were, "Save me, Joe Louis." When The Brown Bomber knocked out Max Schmeling at Yankee Stadium in 1938 in a bout that was considered an allegory of good versus evil, it was the first time that most people had heard a black man referred to simply as "The American."

Meanwhile, Jackie Robinson opened doors for an entire generation of Americans. If there had never been a Jackie Robinson, baseball still would have become integrated; and eventually, other sports would have followed. But that's like saying, if there had been no Michelangelo, someone else would have painted the ceiling of the Sistine Chapel.

Still, Ali's reach, more than that of any of his competitors, was worldwide. So for impact on society, it's Ali (three points), Ruth (two points), and Jordan (one point). That means there's a four-four-four tie, and we go to tie-breakers.

Babe Ruth seemed larger than life. So do Muhammad Ali and Michael Jordan. Ruth and Ali had much-publicized personal weaknesses. Jordan has flaws, although they're less well known. All three men have been idolized. Ali has been loved. It would be presumptuous to choose among them as human beings.

So where do we go from here?

Sixty-four years after Babe Ruth hit his last home run, a half-century after his death, men like Mark McGwire still compete against him. Without Ruth ever having been on *SportsCenter* or HBO, he is still in the hearts of most sports fans. Ali might enjoy that type of recognition fifty years from now. It's less likely that Michael Jordan will.

That brings us down to Babe Ruth and Muhammad Ali.

And the envelope please . . .

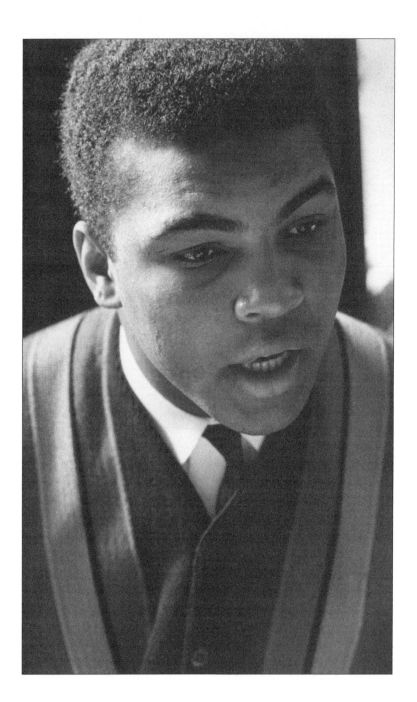

Why Muhammad Ali
Went To Iraq
(1990)

Last month [November 1990] in Baghdad, Muhammad Ali embraced Saddam Hussein and kissed him on the cheek. The moment was televised throughout the world and troubled many people. Ali isn't a diplomat. His actions aren't always wise. There was danger in the possibility that a visit from history's best-known fistic gladiator would feed Hussein's ego and stiffen his resolve. Regardless of what else happened, the meeting would be used for propaganda purposes in the third world, where Ali is particularly loved.

Some of Ali's closest friends were also concerned that, in going to Iraq, he was being used for personal gain by one or more members of his entourage. Several of his associates, past and present, are the subject of a federal inquiry into alleged financial irregularities. While Ali was in Iraq, one of his attorneys was indicted on charges of conspiracy and tax fraud. And among those who accompanied Ali to Baghdad was Arthur Morrison, a self-described businessman who has traversed the United States leaving a trail of arrest warrants behind.

As Ali's trip progressed, it became increasingly difficult for the world outside to distinguish between what he really said and what was reported by the Iraqi News Agency. There were self-appointed spokesmen purporting to act on "hand signals" from the former champion. Others said, falsely, that Ali was unable to speak. But none of this is new to Ali. He has often dealt with con men and crazies.

And the sideshow that accompanied him on his recent journey shouldn't be allowed to overshadow why Ali went to Iraq. It was an act of love in quest of peace. He hoped that his presence would promote dialogue and forestall war.

I've spent the past two years researching and writing about Muhammad Ali. For much of that time, I've lived with him, traveled with him and interviewed hundreds of his family members, associates and friends. I know him well. At least, I think I do. And one thing is certain: even though Muhammad's voice is not as clear as it used to be, his mind is alert and his heart is pure.

I've seen Ali get on a plane and fly to India because the children in an orphanage wanted to meet him. I've sat in his living room as he talked with sadness of hatred and racism in all of their virulent forms. He's a gentle man who will do almost anything to avoid hurting another person.

Ali was in Louisville visiting his mother, who had suffered a stroke when he was asked to go to Iraq. He is on medication for Parkinson's syndrome. When he left that afternoon, he had enough medication with him to last for five days; yet he stayed in Iraq for two weeks. He quite literally endangered his health because he believed that what he was doing was right.

That has been a constant theme throughout Ali's life. He has always taken risks to uphold his principles. During the 1960s, he was stripped of his title and precluded from fighting for three-and-a-half years because he acted upon his beliefs and refused induction into the United States Army during the height of the war in Vietnam. He now believes that all war is wrong. Ali is, and since Vietnam has been, a true conscientious objector.

Ali knows what many of us sometimes seem to forget: that people are killed in wars. Every life is precious to him. He understands that each of us has only one life to live. He is a man who finds it impossible to go hunting, let alone tolerate the horrors of war.

It may be that war with Iraq will become inevitable. If so, it will be fought. But that shouldn't cause us to lose sight of what Muhammad Ali tried to accomplish last month. Any war is a human tragedy, and we should always be thankful for the peacemakers among us.

The Olympic Flame
(1993)

The Atlanta Olympics are three years in the future, but elaborate groundwork has already been laid. Budweiser has agreed to become a national sponsor for a sum that might otherwise be used to retire the national debt. On-site construction has begun, and television planning is underway. Eventually, the Olympic torch will be transported to the United States. And the triumphal procession that follows will lead to the highlight of the Games' opening ceremonies—lighting the Olympic flame.

Traditionally, someone from the host country ignites the flame. At the 1984 Olympics in Los Angeles, Rafer Johnson received the torch and carried it up the Coliseum steps to rekindle the world's most celebrated fire. Last year in Barcelona, a Spanish archer shot an arrow into a caldron, thereby reawakening the flame. The eyes of the world are always on this moment. One wonders who will be chosen to fulfill the honor in Atlanta

The view here is that the choice is obvious. One man embodies the Olympic spirit to perfection. He's a true American in every sense of the word and the foremost citizen of the world. At age eighteen, he won a gold medal in Rome fighting under the name "Cassius Clay." Since then, he has traversed the globe, spreading joy wherever he goes. Atlanta has special meaning for him. It was there, after three years of exile from boxing, that he returned to face Jerry Quarry in the ring. He loves the spotlight, and the spotlight loves him.

So I have a simple proposal to make. I'd like the International Olympic Committee to announce that, as its gift to the world, Muhammad Ali has been chosen to light the Olympic flame in Atlanta. Muhammad has already given us one memorable Olympic moment as Cassius Clay. Now let him share another with the world as Muhammad Ali. That way, the 26th Olympiad will truly be "the greatest."

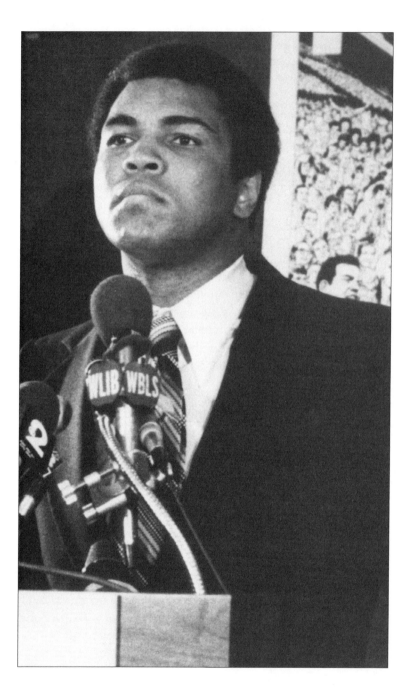

Ali As Diplomat: "No! No! No! Don't!"
(2001)

In 1980, in response to the Soviet Union's invasion of Afghanistan, the Carter Administration sought to organize a boycott of the Moscow Olympics. As part of that effort, it sent Muhammad Ali to five African nations to gather support for America's position.

Ali's trip was a disaster. *Time* magazine later called it, "The most bizarre diplomatic mission in recent U. S. history." Some African officials viewed Ali's presence as a racial insult. "Would the United States send Chris Evert to negotiate with London?" one Tanzanian diplomat demanded. Ali himself seemed confused regarding the facts underlying his role and was unable to explain why African nations should boycott the Moscow Olympics when, four years earlier, the United States had refused to join twenty-nine African countries in boycotting the Montreal Olympics over South Africa's place in the sporting world.

"Maybe I'm being used to do something that ain't right," Ali conceded at one point. In Kenya, he announced that Jimmy Carter had put him "on the spot" and sent him "around the world to take the whupping over American policies," and said that, if he'd known the "whole history of America and South Africa," he "probably wouldn't have made the trip."

That bit of history is relevant now because Jack Valenti (president of the Motion Picture Association of America) has unveiled tentative plans for a one-minute public service announcement featuring Ali that will be broadcast throughout the Muslim world. The thrust of the message is that America's war on terrorism is not a war against Islam. The public service spot would be prepared by Hollywood 9/11—a group that was formed after movie industry executives met on November 11th with Karl Rove (a senior political advisor to George Bush). In Valenti's words, Ali would be held out as "the spokesman for Muslims in America."

The proposed public service announcement might be good publicity for the movie industry, but it's dangerous politics.

Ali is universally respected and loved, but he isn't a diplomat. He doesn't understand the complexities of geopolitics. His heart is pure, but his judgments and actions are at times unwise. An example of this occurred on December 19th at a fundraising event for the proposed Muhammad Ali Center. The center is intended to be an educational facility designed to promote tolerance and understanding among all people. At the fundraiser, Ali rose to tell several jokes.

"No! No! No! Don't," his wife Lonnie cried.

Despite her plea, Ali proceeded. "What's the difference between a Jew and a canoe?" he asked. Then he supplied the answer: "A canoe tips." That was followed by, "A black, a Puerto Rican, and a Mexican are in a car. Who's driving?" The answer? "The police."

Afterward, Sue Carls (a spokesperson for the Ali Center) sought to minimize the damage, explaining, "These are not new jokes. Muhammad tells them all the time because he likes to make people laugh, and he shocks people to make a point." Two days later, Lonnie Ali added, "Even The Greatest can tell bad jokes."

The problem is, this is a situation where misjudgments and bad jokes can cost lives.

Ali is not a bigot. He tells far more "nigger" jokes than jokes about Hispanics and Jews. But Ali sometimes speaks and acts without considering the implications of his words and conduct. And he can be swayed by rhetoric; particularly when the speaker is a Muslim cleric with a following in some portion of the world.

What happens if, six months from now, Ali makes an intemperate statement about Israel? What happens if Ali calls for a halt to all

American military action against terrorism in the heartfelt belief that a halt will save innocent lives? Will he then still be "the spokesman for Muslims in America."

Muhammad Ali leads best when he leads by example and by broad statements in support of tolerance and understanding among all people. To ask more of him in the current incendiary situation is looking for trouble.

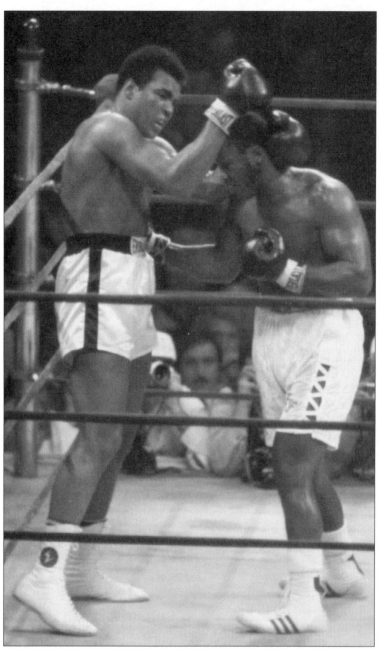

Ali vs Frazier II.

Ghosts of Manila
(2001)

Albert Einstein once remarked, "Nature, to be sure, distributes her gifts unevenly among her children. But it strikes me as unfair, and even in bad taste, to select a few of them for boundless admiration, attributing superhuman powers of mind and character to them."

But society did just that with Muhammad Ali. Few people have ever received accolades equal to those that have been showered upon him. Indeed, Wilfred Sheed, who himself was skeptical of Ali's merit as a social figure, once observed that boxing's eras would be forever known as B.C. (before Clay) and A.D. (Ali Domini).

Enter Mark Kram. Kram is a very good writer. How else can one describe a man who refers to Chuck Wepner as having a face that looks as though it has been "embroidered by a tipsy church lady," and likens Joe Frazier's visage after Ali-Frazier I to "a frieze of a lab experiment that was a disaster." Kram covered boxing for *Sports Illustrated* for eleven years. Now, a quarter-century later, he has written *Ghosts of Manila: The Fateful Blood Feud Between Muhammad Ali and Joe Frazier*. The book, in the first instance, is the story of two men whose rivalry was ugly, glorious, brutal, and enthralling. And secondarily, Kram declares, "This book is intended to be a corrective to the years of stenography that have produced the Ali legend. Cheap myth coruscates the man. The wire scheme for his sculpture is too big."

Thus, Kram seeks to raise Joe Frazier to a level virtually equal to that of Ali in the ring and perhaps above him in terms of character. And in so doing, he portrays what he believes to be the dark side of Ali.

Ghosts of Manila is divided into four parts. They cover, in order, Ali and Frazier in retirement; the emergence of both men as fighters and in the public consciousness; their three fights; and the two men, again, in retirement.

Kram concedes Ali's ring greatness. "As a fighter," Kram writes, "he was the surface of a shield, unmalleable, made for mace and chain, flaring with light." Describing Ali in the ring moments before Ali-Frazier I, he acknowledges, "Whatever you might think of him, you were forced to look at him with honest lingering eyes, for there might never be his like again. Assessed by ring demands—punch, size, speed, intelligence, command, and imagination—he was an action poet, the equal of the best painting you could find."

As for Frazier, Kram calls him "the most skillful devastating inside puncher in boxing history," and goes so far as to rank him among the top five heavyweights of all time. That seems a bit silly. Joe was a great fighter and every bit as noble a warrior as Ali. But there's a time-honored axiom in boxing that styles make fights. And the list of fighters with the style to beat Joe Frazier numbers far more than five.

Kram is on more solid ground when he catalogs Frazier's hatred for Ali. The story of how Muhammad branded Joe an "Uncle Tom" before their first fight, "ignorant" before Ali-Frazier II, and a "gorilla" before Ali-Frazier III is well known, but *Ghosts of Manila* makes it fresh and compelling. Thus, Kram writes, "Muhammad Ali swam inside Joe Frazier like a determined bacillus . . . Ali has sat in Frazier's gut like a broken bottle." And he quotes Frazier's one-time associate Bert Watson as saying, "You don't do to a man what Ali did to Joe. Ali robbed him of who he is. To a lot of people, Joe is still ignorant, slow-speaking, dumb, and ugly. That tag never leaves him. People have only seen one Joe; the one created by Ali. If you're a man, that's going to get to you in a big way." And Kram quotes Frazier as saying of Ali, "When a man gets in your blood like that, you can't never let go. Yesterday is today for me. He'll never die for me . . . If we were twins in the belly of our mama, I'd reach over and strangle him . . . I'll outlive him."

Kram writes with grace and constructs his case against Ali's super-vening greatness in a largely intelligent way. But his work is flawed. First, there are factual inaccuracies. For example, Kram is simply wrong when he discusses Ali's military draft reclassification and states "Had he not become a Muslim, chances are he would have remained unfit for duty." That's not the case. In truth, Ali had been declared unfit for military duty by virtue of his scoring in the sixteenth percentile on an Army intelligence test. That left him well below the requirement of thirty. But two years after that, with the war in Vietnam expanding, the mental-aptitude percentile required by the military was lowered from thirty to fifteen. The change impacted upon hundreds of thousands of young men across the country. To suggest that Ali was somehow singled out and the standard changed because of his religion is ridiculous.

Also, there are times when Kram is overly mean-spirited. For example, Bryant Gumbel (who aroused Kram's ire with negative commentary on Joe Frazier) is referred to as "a mediocre writer and thinker" with "a shallow hard-worked ultra-sophistication and ego that not even a mother could love." Ali in his current condition is labeled "a billboard in decline," of whom Kram says uncharitably, "Physical disaster of his own making has kept his fame intact. He would have become the bore dodged at the party. The future prom-ised that there would be no more clothes with which to dress him up." Indeed, Kram goes so far as to call the younger Ali "a useful idiot" and "near the moronic level."

Kram's failure to distinguish fully between Nation of Islam doctrine and orthodox Islamic beliefs is also troubling. During what might have been the most important fourteen years of Ali's life, he adhered to the teachings of the Nation of Islam; a doctrine that Arthur Ashe later condemned as "a racist ideology, a sort of American apartheid." Yet reading *Ghosts of Manila*, one might come away with the impression that Nation of Islam doctrine was, and still is, Islam as practiced by more than one billion people around the world today. That's because Kram has the annoying habit of referring to Ali's early mentors as "the Muslims," which is like lumping Billy Graham and the Ku Klux Klan together and calling them "the Christians."

Then there's the matter of Kram's sources; most notably, his reliance on two women named Aaisha Ali and Khaliah Ali.

Muhammad met Aaisha Ali in 1973 when he was 31 years old and she was a 17-year-old named Wanda Bolton. To his discredit, they had sexual relations and she became pregnant. Kram makes much of the fact that Wanda was "on her way to becoming a doctor." Given the fact that she was a high school junior at the time, that's rather speculative. Regardless, Ms. Bolton subsequently claimed that she and Ali had been "Islamically married" and changed her name to Aaisha Ali. Muhammad acknowledged paternity and accepted financial responsibility for their daughter, Khaliah.

Kram describes Aaisha several times as "a mystery woman," which is a cheap theatrical trick. Her presence in Ali's past has been known and written about for years. More significantly, Kram uses Aaisha and Khaliah as his primary sources to trash Ali's current wife Lonnie (who Kram calls Ali's "new boss"). Indeed, after describing Ali as "a careless fighter who had his brain cells irradiated," Kram quotes Lonnie as telling Khaliah, "I am Muhammad Ali now." Then, after referring to "Lonnie and her tight circle of pushers," he quotes Khaliah as saying of her father, "It's about money. He's a substance; an item." And after that, Kram recounts a scene when Ali and Lonnie were in a Louisville hospital visiting Ali's mother, who was being kept alive on a respirator. The final days of Odessa Clay's life were the saddest ever for Ali. Yet again, relying wholly on Khaliah, Kram quotes Lonnie as saying, "We can't afford this, Muhammad."

The problem is, there are a lot of people who think that Aaisha Ali and Khaliah Ali aren't particularly reliable sources. I happen to have been present at one of the incidents in which Kram quotes Khaliah. It involved a championship belt that was given to Ali at a dinner commemorating the twentieth anniversary of the first Ali-Frazier fight. The dinner took place on the night of April 14, 1991, although Kram mistakenly reports it as occurring on an unspecified date five years later. Khaliah left Ali's hotel room that night with the belt. I experienced the incident very differently from the way Kram recounts it.

However, my biggest concern regarding *Ghosts of Manila* is its

Ali mocks Frazier's suspenders in 1967.

thesis that Ali's influence lay entirely in the sporting arena. Kram acknowledges that Ali "did lead the way for black athletes out of the frustrating silence that Jackie Robinson had to endure." However, even that concession is tempered by the claim that, "Ali's influence in games today can be seen in the blaring unending marketing of self, the cheap acting out of performers, and the crassness of player interactions. His was an overwhelming presence that, if you care about such things, came at a high cost."

And then Kram goes on to say, "What was laughable, if you knew anything about Ali at all, was that the literati was certain that he was a serious voice, that he knew what he was doing. He didn't have a clue. Seldom has a public figure of such superficial depth been more wrongly perceived."

"Ali," Kram says flatly, "was not a social force." And woe to those who say he was, because their utterances are dismissed as "heavy breathing" from "know-nothings" and "trendy tasters of faux revolution."

Apparently, I'm one of those heavy breathers. Kram refers to me as "a lawyer-Boswell who seems intent of making the public believe that, next to Martin Luther King, Ali is the most important black figure in the last half-century." And in case anyone misses his point, Kram adds, "Current hagiographers have tied themselves in knots trying to elevate Ali into a heroic defiant catalyst of the antiwar movement, a beacon of black independence. It's a legacy that evolves from the intellectually loose sixties, from those who were in school then and now write romance history."

Actually, Kram has misquoted me. I believe he's referring to a statement in *Muhammad Ali: His Life and Times* in which I wrote, "With the exception of Martin Luther King, no black man in America had more influence than Ali during the years when Ali was in his prime." I still believe that to be true.

Was Ali as important as Nelson Mandela? No. Was Ali in the late-1960s more important than any other black person in America except for Dr. King? I believe so. Indeed, Nelson Mandela himself said recently, "Ali's refusal to go to Vietnam and the reasons he gave made him an international hero. The news could not be shut out even by prison walls. He became a real legend to us in prison."

Kram's remarkable gift for words notwithstanding, Muhammad Ali in the 1960s stood as a beacon of hope for oppressed people all over the world. Every time he looked in the mirror and uttered the phrase, "I'm so pretty," he was saying "black is beautiful" before it became fashionable. When he refused induction into the United States Army, regardless of his motives, he stood up to armies around the globe in support of the proposition that, unless you have a very good reason for killing people, war is wrong.

Dick Gregory once said, "If you wanted to do a movie to depict Ali, it would just be a small light getting bigger and bigger and bigger and bigger. That was Ali in a sea of darkness." One can imagine Kram gagging at imagery like that. But the truth is, Muhammad Ali found his way into the world's psyche.

Perhaps Reggie Jackson put it in perspective best. "Do you have any idea what Ali meant to black people?" Jackson told me once. "He was the leader of a nation; the leader of black America. As a young black, at times I was ashamed of my color; I was ashamed of my hair. And Ali made me proud. I'm just as happy being black now as somebody else is being white, and Ali was part of that growing process. Think about it! Do you understand what it did for black Americans to know that the most physically gifted, possibly the most handsome, and one of the most charismatic men in the world was black. Ali helped raise black people in this country out of mental slavery. The entire experience of being black changed for millions of people because of Ali."

In sum, Muhammad Ali might not have meant much to Mark Kram. But he meant a great deal to a lot of people. He made an enormous difference.

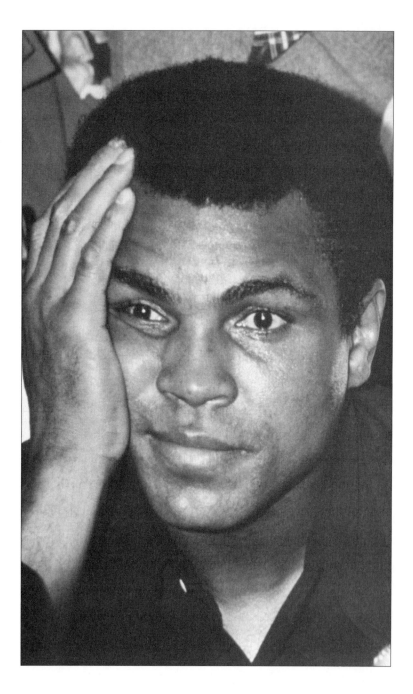

A Holiday Season
Fantasy
(2004)

In the 1960s and '70s, Muhammad Ali's most important contribution was to force an understanding of the divisions between black and white in American society and, ultimately, to help bridge that gap. Now there's a more-threatening chasm: the horrible hatred that exists between the Islamic and non-Islamic world.

Ali is only one man. But he might be the most recognized and most loved person on the planet. He has a reservoir of good will that draws upon the love and good feeling that he has earned from all races, all nationalities, and all religions.

More than a decade ago, Ali told me, "I got a plan. Someday I'm gonna hitchhike from New York to California with no money, no clothes except what I'm wearing, nothing. Then I'm going from California over to Asia, and from Asia to Europe and Africa and South America. I'm going all around the world with just my face to see how people greet me and take care of me. I could go just about any place in the world, knock on any door, and people would know me and let me in. I might even march on foot through Egypt, Israel, Lebanon, all them countries, and tell people to stop fighting and agree on a peace that's fair to everyone. Some people say that might be dangerous, but you gotta take risks. Columbus discovered America by sailing around the world when people thought he'd fall off. We got men on the moon by risking their lives."

It's only a fantasy. But what if Muhammad Ali were to walk

through the troubled regions of the world today on a year-long journey to promote tolerance and understanding among all people?

It would be a dream-like quest. But Ali is a dreamer, as were Mahatma Gandhi and Nelson Mandela when they began their journeys.

Would it be dangerous? Absolutely. But Ali was one of the most reviled people in America in the 1960s. It was a decade of assassinations in the United States. John F. Kennedy, Robert Kennedy, and Malcolm X were all shot down. How did Muhammad respond to the threat?

"I'm an easy target," Ali said in 1965. "I'm everywhere; everybody knows me. I walk the streets daily and nobody's guarding me. I have no guns, no police. So if someone's gonna get me, tell them to come on and get it over with; if they can get past God, because God is controlling the bullet."

If Ali undertook a walk for peace, it would be the modern equivalent of the wanderings described in the holy books of the world.

The journey could begin with a statement: "I'm embarking on this undertaking as a way of speaking out against the hatred and violence that imperil the world. I'm not going to talk about political issues. I'm not going to take sides. I'm going to embrace every person I meet regardless of that person's religion, color, or ideology. My presence will speak for itself. My message is simple. Killing is wrong. Hating is wrong. Every person is deserving of love. Whatever happens to me on this journey, I want no blood shed or prejudice voiced at any time ever in my name."

To be successful, Ali's journey would have to be independent of governments and any other entity, religious or otherwise, no matter how well-intentioned that group might be. There would be no spin-masters; no spokespeople; no prearranged meetings with selected groups. It would be one man walking where he chose to walk; speaking without words; telling every person he met by virtue of his presence that hate has to be cleansed from peoples' hearts one person at a time.

In his inaugural speech, John F. Kennedy declared, "Let us go forth to lead the land we love, asking His blessing and His help, but knowing that, here on Earth, God's work must truly be our own."

Were Ali to undertake the journey described above, he would truly be doing "God's work." He would be a prophet of peace.

But it's just a fantasy.

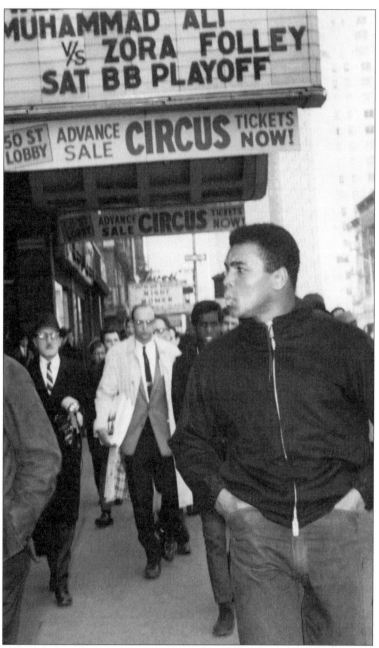

A stroll before a Garden showdown with Folley.

PERSONAL MEMORIES

Ali stares at Zora Folley during their 1967 weigh-in.

The Day I Met Muhammad Ali

(2005)

In September 1964, when I was a sophomore at Columbia University, I began hosting a radio show called *Personalities In Sports* for the student-run radio station. For an 18-year-old sports fan, it was heady stuff. Each week, I'd take a bulky reel-to-reel tape recorder into the field and interview the biggest names I could get. I reached Nirvana one afternoon when I found myself in the New York Yankees dugout as the Bronx Bombers readied to nail down their fourteenth pennant in sixteen years. The first interview I conducted was with Tom Tresh. Whitey Ford was next. Then Mickey Mantle entered the dugout and, gathering my courage, I approached him.

"Mr. Mantle. My name is Tom Hauser, and I wonder if I could interview you for WKCR."

"Fuck."

That was all Mantle said. Not even "fuck you." Just "fuck," which I assumed meant "no," since he then turned and walked away from me.

Recovering from the rebuff, I moved on to Elston Howard, Jim Bouton, and Johnny Keane. My final interview was with Ralph Terry. I asked who he was planning to vote for in the upcoming presidential election between Lyndon Johnson and Barry Goldwater. Terry told me that his political views were none of my business, and the interview ended on that note.

The following week, I had similar success with New York Mets pitcher Tracy Stallard. Three years earlier, while on the mound for the Boston Red Sox, Stallard had earned a place in baseball history by throwing home run number sixty-one to Roger Maris. I suggested to Stallard that he tell WKCR's listeners all about it, and he responded, "I think you know all about it, and your listeners know all about it, and I don't want to talk about it."

Regardless, over the next thirty months, I taped dozens of interviews. New York Knicks center Walter Bellamy gave me the first great quote I ever got from an athlete, when I asked about reports that he'd had a bad attitude while playing for the Baltimore Bullets. "I've never known an attitude to go up and dunk a basketball," Bellamy told me. Joe Namath, who'd just signed a three-year contract with the New York Jets for the unheard-of sum of $427,000 spread over ten years talked at length about the transition from college to pro football. Pete Rozelle and Joe Foss (commissioners of the warring National and American football leagues) gave of their time. Wills Reed, Barry Kramer, Eddie Donovan, Tom Gola, Matt Snell, Weeb Eubank. The list went on . . .

With one particularly memorable moment.

In March 1967, Muhammad Ali was preparing to fight Zora Folley at "the old" Madison Square Garden; that is, the arena on Eighth Avenue between 49th and 50th Streets. The bout was scheduled for March 22nd, forty-four days after Ali's brutalization of Ernie Terrell. At that point in his career, Ali was virtually unbeatable. This would be his seventh championship defense in less than a year. Folley was a decent human being and a respected journeyman, who'd been a professional fighter for fifteen years.

John Condon, the director of publicity for Madison Square Garden, arranged the interview for me. Ali-Folley would be the last heavyweight championship fight at the old Garden and also Ali's final bout before a three-and-a-half-year exile from boxing. The war in Vietnam was at its peak. The National Selective Service Presidential Appeal Board had voted unanimously to maintain Muhammad's 1-A classification, and he'd been ordered to report for induction in April. The assumption was that he would refuse induction. Ali himself had hinted as much when he said, "Why should they ask me to put on a uniform and go ten thousand miles from home and drop bombs on brown people in Vietnam, while so-called Negro people in Louisville are treated like dogs?"

At the Garden, I watched Ali go through a series of exercises. Then I stood at the edge of the ring as he sparred with Jimmy Ellis. When that was done, he went into his dressing room and I followed. John Condon introduced us. Ali was wearing a white terrycloth robe. I wasn't from *The New York Times* or any other news organization of note, but that didn't seem to matter. Ali told me to turn on my tape recorder. We talked mostly about Nation of Islam doctrine, with some questions about the military draft, Zora Folley, and boxing in general thrown in. It's a sign of the times that both of us used the word "Negro." Ten minutes after we began, Ali announced, "That's all I'm gonna do," and the interview was over.

But I had one more request. An autograph. Not for me, but for my younger brother, who loved sports every bit as much as I did. Earlier in the year, he'd given me a copy of a book entitled *Black Is Best: The Riddle of Cassius Clay*. Now, I wanted to give the book back to him. As I looked on, Ali inscribed the titled page:

> To Jim Hauser
> From Muhammad Ali
> World Heavyweight Champion
> Good luck
> 1967

I still remember the look on Jim's face when I gave it to him.

While Ali took a shower, I taped an interview with Angelo Dundee. Then I returned to the ring, where Zora Folley was finishing his sparring session. Folley told me how he planned to exploit the fact that Ali held his hands too low and backed away from punches instead of slipping them. The interviews aired on the night of the fight. For the first time ever, *The New York Times* listings for radio programs of interest cited *Personalities In Sports* and yours truly by name.

Years later, I would come in contact with John Condon again. In 1984, I was researching a book entitled *The Black Lights: Inside the World of Professional Boxing*. Condon had become president of

Madison Square Garden Boxing; and with characteristic generosity, he opened doors on my behalf. Our final meeting came in 1989. As fate would have it, Ali and I had also moved full circle by then. I'd been chosen to be his official biographer and was in the process of writing *Muhammad Ali: His Life and Times*. Condon was one of two hundred people I interviewed for the project. He was dying of cancer and knew it. At the close of our interview, John gave me a copy of *Black Is Best: The Riddle of Cassius Clay* that had been on a shelf in his office for more than twenty years. "Keep it," he told me. "I won't be needing it any longer." That night, I listened to the tape of my WKCR radio interview with Ali for the first time in more than two decades.

Eventually, of course, I played the tape for Ali. One night when he was at my apartment for dinner, I took my old reel-to-reel tape recorder out of the closet and turned it on.

About a minute into the interview, Muhammad reached into the formidable sack of one-liners that he carries with him at all times. "I remember that afternoon," he said. "You were wearing a blue shirt."

"And you were wearing a white terrycloth robe."

We listened to the rest of the tape in silence. Then Ali queried, "Was I really wearing a white terrycloth robe?"

"Yes. Was I really wearing a blue shirt?"

Ali laughed. "You're crazy," he said.

Transcript of March 1967 Radio Interview
Conducted by Thomas Hauser with Muhammad Ali

Q: Your outlook on life is different from that of a great many other people. It's based on your religion. Could you give us some idea of what it is?

ALI: As far as my outlook is concerned, I'd say that ninety percent of the American public feels just the way I do as far as racial issues are concerned; as far as intermarriage is concerned; forced integration and total integration such as many Negro civil rights groups are trying to accomplish today. We who follow the Honorable Elijah Muhammad don't believe that this is the solution to our problem. Unity among self, respect for self, doing for self is what we believe. And this don't make me no different from whites, because the masses of them believe and have been practicing this ever since we've been in America. So my outlook on life is really the same as ninety percent of the whites in America. They're just shocked and surprised to see that we the Negro who have accepted the teachings of Elijah Muhammad now want to be with ourselves and live among ourselves and don't want to force integrate, and that's such a surprise to the whites, which makes us controversial and different but really we're not different. We're just different from the Negro who's striving for forced integration. But as a whole, the whites believe like we do and have been believing like we do all the time.

Q: Would you like to see a world someday where the white man and Negro can live together and call each other friends?

ALI: I'm not the one to say. I would like to see peace on earth. If separation will bring it, I say let's separate. If integration will bring it, I say let's integrate. But let's not just stand still, where one man holds another in bondage and deprives him of freedom, justice, and equality, neither integrating or letting him go to self. I don't like that. But I like seeing peace, whatever means will bring it.

Q: Do you think the Negro is better than the white man or just different? Are we the same underneath the skin?

ALI: Nobody on earth is made the same. Some are born blind; some crippled; some are yellow; some are red; some are black; some are white. No men are really equal or the same. As far as going into the differences and why they're different, I couldn't say. But the man that we follow for all of our spiritual teachings, who gives us knowledge and understanding, is Elijah Muhammad. And I'm sure that, if you have him on your radio show, he can tell you why we are not alike and dig into the depths of why we're different. But it's not my job to know who's who and who's different, because I'm not that wise. That's up to Elijah Muhammad, our leader.

Q: You've had an outstanding boxing career; perhaps the most outstanding of anyone in the ring today. Who's the toughest opponent you've had to face?

ALI: The toughest opponent I've had to face is Sonny Liston.

Q: What about Floyd Patterson?

ALI: He was easy.

Q: You've said that, in the ring, you tried to humiliate Floyd Patterson and Ernie Terrell. Is that true?

ALI: Yes.

Q: Why?

ALI: Because they talked about me and my religion; mocked my leader and teacher and advisors; and didn't want to respect me as Muhammad Ali, which is my name now. So they're lucky they got off as easy as they did.

Q: Do you think that two wrongs make a right? Was it right to humiliate them like that?

ALI: Is it right to go to war? Is it right that we're in a war now, killing people? I have my beliefs, and I'll defend them.

Q: One of the things that people are interested in now is your status with the draft. What will you do if your final appeals fall through and you're drafted? Will you then resist going into the Army?

ALI: I don't think it would be respectful to the draft board or the government or the Justice Department to make a decision now. That's a hypothetical question. I haven't been drafted yet. My appeals haven't run out. It's in the hands of my lawyer; he's handling it. So it wouldn't be respectful to make a decision or say anything on this radio show. But the world knows that I am a Muslim. The world knows that I'm a sincere follower to death of Elijah Muhammad. And we say five times a day in our prayers, "My prayers, my sacrifices, my life, and my death are all for Allah." I repeat, "My prayers, my sacrifices, my life, and my death are all for Allah." This is what I sincerely believe. I've upheld my faith through the past years. I gave up one of the prettiest Negro women in the country; cost me one-hundred-seventy thousand dollars in alimony. This was all controversy and publicity before the draft started. The white businessmen of Louisville, Kentucky, will tell you that I've turned down eight million dollars in movie contracts, recordings, promotions, and advertisements because of my faith. So I don't see why I should break the rules of my faith now.

Q: There seems to be an opinion circulating that Zora Folley is just here for a pay-day for himself and for you and to keep you in shape. Do you think that Folley represents a genuine threat?

ALI: These are just the hypocrites and the phonies; the newspaper writers that are shook up because everything that I said would come true did come true. I said that I was the greatest. They thought I was just acting the fool. Now instead of admitting that I'm the greatest and admitting that I'm the best heavyweight in all history, they'd rather belittle the contenders and say it's just a pushover. They were complaining because Patterson didn't fight but once a year. They were complaining because Liston didn't fight but once a year. They were complaining because [Ingemar] Johansson didn't fight but once a year. The game was dead. Now I revive it, fighting every two months. And what more can I do but fight the number-one contender. Zora Folley is the number-one man on Earth next to me. So they can call him a bum. They can call him an old man. All I say is, "If he's a bum, if he's an old man, then why do the boxing authorities in this country rank him number one?" So they're just looking for fault, and they don't know what to do. They're all shook up. They said Terrell would be tough; they built him up to be tough. He was nothing. They said Patterson would be tough. He was nothing. They said Cleveland Williams would be a big test. He was nothing. They said Chuvalo would be nothing. He was tough. So don't pay attention to the critics in the press. They don't know nothing about boxing. They never trained a day in their life. They can't throw a left jab. All they can do is talk. They've been wrong, and I've been right. I look for Zora Folley to be tougher than Ernie Terrell.

Q: Who among the young fighters such as Joe Frazier, Buster Mathis, and Jerry Quarry do you look for to give you the most trouble in the years ahead?

ALI: I'd say Joe Frazier.

Q: What does he have that would make him tougher than the others?

ALI: He's strong; he hits hard. I've never really seen none of them fight. But from what I hear, he'd be the toughest.

Q: Have you given any thought to retirement?

ALI: Not really. I believe I'll just stay here and keep whupping them until they find somebody who can whup me.

Q: What sort of long-range plans do you have for when you finish up in the ring?

ALI: I want to be a minister for the Islamic faith as taught by the Honorable Elijah Muhammad. That's all I want to be is a minister.

Frazier vs Ali I.

I Was At Ali-Frazier I
(2005)

I was an ardent sports fan when I was young. I played a lot of baseball, football, and basketball. Those were also my favorite sports to watch. I followed boxing but without the intense interest in the sweet science that I have today.

Like many Americans, I became aware of Cassius Marcellus Clay Jr. at the 1960 Rome Olympics. I found him charming and followed his career as he rose to conquer Sonny Liston. Then, like a lot of people, I was turned off by his adherence to Nation of Islam ideology. The lure of Muhammad Ali's personality was strong, and I had no problem with his message of empowerment for black Americans. But I took issue with the notion that white people were devils who had been created 6,600 years ago by an evil scientist named Mr. Yakub and that apartheid was a preferred way of life. Regardless, in 1967, Ali won me over again when he refused induction into the United States Army during the height of the war in Vietnam.

In 1970, I graduated from Columbia Law School and began clerking for a federal judge prior to a five-year stint as a litigator on Wall Street. The United States Supreme Court had yet to rule on Ali's appeal of his conviction for refusing induction and he was facing five years in prison.

Then, in early 1971, I read that Ali and Joe Frazier had signed to fight at Madison Square Garden. Obviously, it would be a memorable athletic competition. Two great fighters; each one undefeated with a legitimate claim to the heavyweight championship of the world. But just as clearly, it was going to be an event that transcended sports.

The tumultuous decade just passed had been marked by assassinations, men landing on the moon, and the rise of a new drug culture. But its most important markers were Black America rising to assert itself and opposition to the war in Vietnam. Ali symbolized both of those markers.

Joe Frazier, by contrast, was perceived as a symbol of the ruling order. Fairly or unfairly, as Bryant Gumbel later wrote, "Frazier became an instrument of the oppressors. The blackest man in the ring was cast as the villain to blacks across the land and was called hero and savior by the most bigoted of white men."

Tickets for Ali-Frazier I were priced from $20 to $150. The day they went on sale, I bought two mezzanine seats at $20 apiece. On fight night, scalpers were getting ten times those numbers.

I went to the fight with a friend. Entering the Garden, I bought an "official program." It was a generic publication with a LeRoy Neiman painting of Ali and Frazier on the cover and a 16-page insert on "The Fight."

I'd been to Madison Square Garden for boxing once before, but this night was different from its predecessor. Early in Ali's career, Budd Schulberg wrote, "Cassius Marcellus Clay is doing for fistic glamour what Marilyn Monroe did for sex." Now the Garden was glamour personified.

The arena was jammed; there was electricity in the air. Major superstars who were used to sitting on camera in the first row were fifteen rows from ringside and happy to be in the Garden at all. Frank Sinatra wangled a press credential by agreeing to photograph the fight for *Life Magazine*. Thousands of fans stood outside the arena just to be there and watch the celebrities come in.

None of the preliminary fights was slated for more than six rounds. The most notable undercard bout featured Ali's brother, Rahaman, against Danny McAlinden.

Rahaman had fought on the undercard of both Ali-Liston fights and Ali versus Oscar Bonavena. His record stood at 7 wins and 0 losses with 2 knockouts. McAlinden was a heavyweight from Ireland via England. His record was 14-1-2 with 13 KOs, and he had never fought off the sceptered isle before.

Fights in New York were scored at that time on a round-by-round basis, not on points. McAlinden won a majority decision: 4-2, 3-2-1, 3-3.

As the night wore on, the tension grew.

Then, finally, it was time.

"I've covered sports for a half-century," Jerry Izenberg later reminisced. "I've been to every kind of championship and seen every great athlete of the past fifty years. And no moment I've ever seen had the electricity of Muhammad Ali and Joe Frazier coming down the aisle and entering the ring that night."

People forget how young Ali and Frazier were at the time. Muhammad was 29 and Joe only 27. But even though some of Ali's greatest ring triumphs lay in the future, as a fighter he was already growing old.

I watched the action through binoculars. The fight was even in the early rounds, and the crowd evenly divided. But as the night wore on, Frazier partisans had more reason to cheer.

I remember Ali going to the ropes, beckoning Frazier in. I remember round eleven, when Joe wobbled Muhammad with a big left hook. And most painfully, I remember the fifteenth round, when Joe hit Muhammad as hard as a man can be hit and Ali went down. At that point, the fight was lost and my hope was that Muhammad would be able to finish on his feet. He did, although the judges ruled against him: 11-4, 9-6, and 8-6-1.

Ali had been defeated in his first "superfight." Against Sonny Liston in 1964, Cassius Clay had been widely perceived as nothing more than a kid coming to get beaten up. And Ali-Liston II drew only two thousand paying fans. Now, when it mattered most and the world truly cared, "The Greatest" had failed.

I left Madison Square Garden that night feeling depressed but knowing that I had witnessed something historic.

Reflections On Time Spent With Ali

(Combined pieces written from 1991 through 1997)

My personal relationship with Muhammad Ali began in 1988, when we met in New York to explore the possibility of my writing the book that ultimately became *Muhammad Ali: His Life and Times*.

The idea originated with Muhammad's wife, Lonnie, who wanted a book which would place Muhammad in context, not just as a fighter but also as a social, political, and religious figure. I was approached because I had previously written a book about professional boxing entitled *The Black Lights*, as well as books about race relations, public education, United States foreign policy, and a number of other subjects of concern to Muhammad.

On paper, the fit between us seemed good. I was 42 years old, only four years younger than Ali, so I'd experienced his era, from the civil rights movement to the rock music he loves. I'd spent five years as a lawyer on Wall Street, and thus was able to work my way through the financial entanglements of Muhammad's life and the complex litigation that followed his refusal to accept induction into the United States Army. And while I was determined to maintain my objectivity in writing, I was a lifelong Ali fan.

Writing a biography about a living subject is an extremely personal endeavor, and I wanted to make sure that, if the project went ahead, Muhammad and I would get along. I also wanted to make sure that I could capture Muhammad's voice. At the time,

Mike Tyson was the undefeated undisputed heavyweight champion of the world. Some experts were going so far as to proclaim that Tyson was better than Ali in his prime. Thus, before I met with Muhammad and Lonnie, I spent an afternoon writing a piece entitled *I'm Coming Back To Whup Mike Tyson's Butt.* Then, when we got together, I read the piece aloud and presented it to Muhammad. His response was to take a pen from his pocket and write across the front page, "To Tom Hauser from Muhammad Ali—This is what I can still do to Tyson right now."

But there was another threshold issue to confront. Like millions of admirers, I'd seen Muhammad on television. Sometimes he'd looked well. Other times, though, the light seemed all but gone from his eyes. I didn't want to involve myself with the project unless Muhammad was capable of making a significant contribution to it. Also, I didn't want to spend several years working on a book that would be a source of depression instead of joy.

To resolve those issues, after meeting initially with Muhammad and his wife, I accepted their invitation to spend five days at their home in Berrien Springs, Michigan. My first two days there, I was intimidated by Ali's presence. I found it hard to make eye contact with him. Other than John F. Kennedy, who was my boyhood hero, I don't think there's a person on the planet who would have affected me in that manner; certainly not to that extent. Then, on the third morning, I went downstairs to the kitchen. Muhammad was sitting at the breakfast table, finishing his cereal and toast. He looked up and asked if I wanted cornflakes or granola. And in that moment, I realized that any distance between us was my own fault. Muhammad didn't want to be put on a pedestal. He wanted me to relate to him the same way I'd relate to anyone else.

I also realized over time that, despite Ali's speech difficulties, his health is better than most people think it is. Muhammad suffers from Parkinson's syndrome, which refers to a series of symptoms, the most noticeable of which are slurred speech, stiffness in walking, and an occasional facial "mask." The most common cause of Parkinson's syndrome is Parkinson's disease. In Ali's case, the symptoms were brought on by repeated blows to the head; blows that destroyed cells in his brain stem which produce a substance called dopamine. But the condition is not life-threatening. And more important, it's a motor-skills problem. There are no intellectual deficits. Muhammad's wit is sharp, and his thought processes are clear. Indeed, when we signed our contract for me to write the book, I couldn't resist saying, "Muhammad, stick with me and I'll make you famous." And Ali countered, "More famous than Elvis Presley?"

In short, Muhammad doesn't feel sorry for himself because of his physical condition, and there's no reason for anyone else to feel sorry for him. He loves being Muhammad Ali, and he's as happy with each day as anybody I know.

As for the process of researching Ali's life, I proceeded on several levels. First, there were Muhammad's personal papers, medical records, newspapers, magazines, tapes, and cartons of legal and financial documents. After that, I interviewed approximately two hundred people—members of Ali's family, friends, former wives, ring opponents, business associates, doctors, world leaders, and others who have known him best. And of course, there were countless days spent with Muhammad. I traveled with him around the world, spent weeks in his home, and entertained him in mine.

One of my memories is of waking up one morning in the Ali's home in Berrien Springs and hearing Lonnie cry out, "Oh my God! Muhammad! What have you done?"

Naturally, I was curious. So I put on my clothes, went downstairs, and found Lonnie standing in the living room amidst piles of clothes, boxes, and other belongings. Apparently, during the night, Muhammad had been unable to sleep. As he often does under those circumstances, he'd gone downstairs to read the Qur'an. Then, for reasons known only to him, he'd grown curious as to what was in the closets. And the easiest way to satisfy that curiosity was to empty all of them out onto the living room floor. Suffice it to say that Lonnie assumed it was Muhammad (and not me) who had done the deed.

Unlike Ali's earlier biographers, I enjoyed total access to Muhammad and to virtually all of the key people in his life. My questions were answered with candor by almost everyone. And I enjoyed the advantage of perspective, since I was writing at a time when Ali's ring career and the tumultuous era of American history that went with it had come to an end.

Inevitably, writing the book involved revisiting my own youth. It led me to recall watching the 1960 Olympics on television, and reading newspapers in high school for reports of Cassius Clay's early fights. I reexperienced listening to the radio as a 17-year-old college freshman the night Clay beat Sonny Liston for the heavyweight championship. The war in Vietnam; assassinations; riots in Newark, Harlem, and Watts. In one way or another, so many of the key events in American history that I remembered were intertwined with Ali's life. And I relived sitting in a New York theater on October 2, 1980, turning my face away from the screen to avoid watching the brutalization of an aging Ali at the hands of Larry Holmes.

In some ways, Ali is a very simple man. In others, he's quite complex. But first and foremost, Muhammad is deeply religious and spiritual. There was a time when he molded his religious beliefs to accommodate what he wanted to do. Now, though, it's the other way around. I don't think I've met anybody ever who is more sincere about his religious principles than Muhammad. God is the main factor in his life. At the end of each day, Ali asks himself, "If God were to judge me based just on what I did today, would I go to heaven or hell?" And he lives his life accordingly. "I'm not afraid of dying," Ali told me once. "I have faith; I do everything I can to live my life right; and I believe that dying will bring me closer to God."

Yet Muhammad has never sought to impose his religious beliefs on other people. Indeed, once when I accompanied him to services at a mosque to share that part of his life, he told me, "When we say our Islamic prayers, you can say your Jewish prayers. Only don't say them out loud because it might offend someone."

I also recall another moment between us that turned on Muhammad's religious beliefs. One day, we were discussing Ali's 1976 "autobiography." The book contains numerous allegorical tales, including the claim that young Cassius Clay threw his Olympic gold medal into the Ohio River after being denied service at a segregated restaurant.

"You didn't really do that, did you?" I queried.

"Yes, I did."

"Swear to Allah."

There was no response.

"Swear to Allah," I pressed.

"Someone stole it," Ali admitted. "Or I lost it."

Ali is a kind man, who speaks often of his dreams and never of his troubles. Those who meet him are virtually never disappointed. He has an endurance and tolerance for others that's extraordinary. He's forgiving, perhaps even to a fault. There are people who have stolen literally millions of dollars from him. He knows they've done it, yet he refuses to say one word against them. To some, that means he's a soft touch. To others, he has a tender heart. Ali himself says only, "God is merciful and forgiving, so I should be too." Also, once in a reflective moment, he told me, "Maybe I should say more about certain things. Sometimes I don't say what I feel, because God gave me so much power that I'm afraid, if I yell at someone, it will hurt them too much." That might be Ali's way of avoiding personal confrontations; an avoidance he too often seeks. But it's also a mark of considerable character.

Ali sometimes makes mistakes. There's an irrational side to his personality. At times he's manipulated and easily led. But his heart is pure; he loves people. And that love manifests itself every day; if not on a world stage, then in his private life. In November 1990, against the advice of some of his closest friends, Muhammad journeyed to Iraq to meet with Saddam Hussein in the hope that his presence would forestall war in the Persian Gulf. Afterward, I asked if he thought it was wise to have gone. And Ali answered, "People risk their lives for war all the time. Why shouldn't I risk mine for peace." Meanwhile, three months later, away from the glare of publicity, Muhammad and Lonnie Ali quietly adopted a six-week-old boy.

"That's a very lucky little boy," I told him. "You've changed the course of his entire life."

"We're lucky too," Muhammad answered. "It's a good baby."

There are so many memories I have of Ali that conjure up a smile. Once, when Muhammad and I got in his car to do some errands, he told me, "You get in back; I'll drive, and it will be like *Driving Miss Daisy*."

Joe Frazier and Muhammad Ali in 1970.

On another occasion, when Ali and his wife were coming to my apartment for dinner, I invited one of his favorite rock stars—Chubby Checker, who lives in Philadelphia—to join us. Chubby drove ninety miles to New York. When Ali saw him, he started jumping up and down, shouting, "It's Chubby Checker! It's Chubby Checker!" But what touched me most about that evening was an exchange that came after dinner. We were sitting in the living room. Muhammad looked at Chubby and asked, "Did you drive all the way from Philadelphia just to see me?" Chubby said yes. And Ali responded, shaking his head, "I can't believe it. I'm honored."

I researched and wrote *Muhammad Ali: His Life and Times* for two years. Finally, in September 1990, I journeyed again to Berrien Springs to meet with Muhammad, Lonnie, and Howard Bingham. For ten days, we read every word of my manuscript aloud. By agreement, there was to be no censorship. The purpose of our reading was to ensure that the book would be factually accurate.

There were portions of the manuscript that troubled Muhammad because they reflected negatively on persons other than himself. Also, it was important to him that the book be accurate with regard to all facets of Islam. As for his first concern, ultimately he understood that it was important for the story of his life to be told honestly and completely. With respect to the latter, a careful reading of the manuscript by Dr. Ibrahim Oweiss, a leading Islamic scholar, put Ali's worries to rest.

At one point during our reading of the manuscript, I quoted some particularly harsh words from Joe Frazier. "I hated Ali," Joe said. "God might not like me talking that way, but it's in my heart. Twenty years, I've been fighting Ali, and I still want to take him apart piece by piece and send him back to Jesus."

Then the words got harsher. "He shook me in Manila," Joe acknowledged. "He won. But I sent him home worse than he came. Look at him now. He's damaged goods. I know it; you know it. Everyone knows it; they just don't want to say it. He was always making fun of me. I'm the dummy. I'm the one getting hit in the head. Tell me now. Him or me, which one talks worse now? He can't talk no more and he still tries to make noise."

There was a silent moment.

"Did you hear that, Muhammad?" Lonnie asked.

Ali nodded.

"How do you feel, knowing that hundreds of thousands of people will read that?

"It's what he said," Ali answered.

Meanwhile, the moment I remember best from our final sessions in Berrien Springs came when Lonnie was reading a quotation from television boxing analyst Alex Wallau. Wallau had expressed the view that, even if Ali had been given foreknowledge of how boxing would affect his physical condition, "If he had it to do all over, he'd live his life the same way; he'd still choose to be a fighter."

As soon as Lonnie read those words, Muhammad sat up straight in his chair and said, "You bet I would."

Muhammad Ali: His Life and Times was published in 1991. Muhammad helped promote the book and, among other things, attended book signings at Barnes & Noble and Waldenbooks stores in New York. Each signing was enormously successful. Both stores reported that Ali sold more books in a single session than any previous subject or author.

The final promotional event in New York was Ali's attendance at the annual Boxing Writers Association of America dinner. Muhammad spoke briefly, and told the audience about a slave named Omar. It was a parable that preached the message of humility and was met by sustained applause. Then Ali sat down; the program resumed. And HBO's Jim Lampley was speaking, when suddenly Muhammad returned to the podium and announced, "I forgot to tell you. I had two book signings this week, and I broke the all-time record at both stores."

That left Lampley to wonder aloud, "Muhammad, would Omar the slave brag about his book signings?"

"He would if he sold a thousand books," Muhammad countered.

Eventually, *Muhammad Ali: His Life and Times* was published in Great Britain, and we journeyed to England for a book tour. One afternoon, I was sitting next to Ali at a book signing in London, when a woman in her forties passed through the line. She looked at Muhammad, then at me, and in a thick Irish accent asked, "Excuse me, are you Ali's son?"

"No, ma'am," I replied.

"Oh," she said with obvious disappointment. "You look just like him."

My initial reaction was to dismiss her as daft. After all, I'm white and only four years younger than Muhammad. But then it occurred to me that this was one more example of how, when it comes to Ali, people are colorblind. And of course, it's a compliment of the highest order to be told that you look just like Muhammad Ali.

As our tour of England continued, there were also poignant moments. Late one afternoon, we found ourselves in Nottingham. It had been a long day. That morning, we'd been in Leeds, where Muhammad had signed nine hundred books, posed for photographs, kissed babies, and shaken hands with literally thousands of admirers. Now that scene was being repeated with five hundred more people who had waited in line for hours for their hero to arrive.

Ali was tired. He'd been awake since 5:00 a.m., when he'd risen to pray and read from the Qur'an. His voice, already weak from the ravages of Parkinson's syndrome, was flagging. And the facial "mask" which accompanies his medical condition was more pronounced than usual.

Most of the people in line were joyful. But one of them, a middle-aged woman with a kind face, wasn't. Muhammad's condition grieved her and, as she approached him, she burst into tears.

Ali leaned over, kissed her on the cheek, and told her, "Don't feel bad. God has blessed me. I've had a good life, and it's still good. I'm having fun now."

The woman walked away smiling. For the rest of her life, she would remember meeting Ali. Moments later, she turned to look back at him, but Muhammad's attention was already focused on the next person in line, a tall handsome black man. "You're uglier than Joe Frazier," Ali told him.

That brings us again to Joe. Of all Muhammad's ring opponents, the only one who still holds a grudge against him is Frazier. Joe makes no secret of his dislike for Muhammad, and sometimes his antipathy extends to Muhammad's friends. In recent years, Joe and I have gotten along fairly well. He's been a guest in my home and he's cordial when we meet. But it wasn't always that way.

In 1991, I was in Atlantic City for a WBO heavyweight championship bout between Ray Mercer and Tommy Morrison. Frazier was in attendance, and I introduced him to a friend of mine named Neil Ragin.

Joe's response was a resounding, "Grhummpf!"

"It's nothing against you," I explained to Neil. "Joe doesn't talk to me a whole lot."

Which gave Neil a chance to ingratiate himself to Joe and keep the conversation going. "Of course, Joe doesn't talk with you. You're Ali's man. Everybody knows you're Ali's man. Right, Joe?"

Whereupon Joe said simply, "Right! And I ain't talking to you either, 'cause you the friend of Ali's man."

Muhammad told me once, "If Joe Frazier wants to forgive and forget, I'll be friends. And if he wants to fight, I'm still whuppin' him." Then, on a more serious note, he added, "Joe Frazier is a good man. I couldn't have done what I did without him, and he couldn't have done what he did without me. If God ever calls me to a holy war, I want Joe Frazier fighting beside me."

Still, I have to say, even today, if Ali and Frazier were together and Joe had a balloon, Muhammad would want to pop it. And when it comes to Joe, Muhammad still gives as good as he gets. Once, I was with them at a ceremony at the United Nations. Ali's son, Asaad, who was a year old, was also there. And Joe was looking for trouble. Smiling at Asaad, he told onlookers, "Hmmm, that boy looks just like me."

And Ali didn't miss a beat. "Don't call my boy ugly," he said.

During the time I spent with Ali, he was constantly creating new memories and generating "new material." For example, we were in Seattle to attend a dinner where Muhammad was honored as "The Fighter of the Century." The festivities included a fight card at The Kingdome. Meeting Ali, the undercard fighters were in awe. One of them, a lightweight with a losing record in a handful of professional bouts, went so far as to confess, "Mr. Ali, I just want you to know, when I'm going to the ring for a fight, I get real nervous; so I say to myself, 'I'm Muhammad Ali; I'm the greatest fighter of all time, and no one can beat me.'"

Ali leaned toward the fighter and whispered, "When I was boxing and got nervous before a fight, I said the same thing."

"If you do roadwork in the snow, it makes you tough," another young fighter told Muhammad.

"If you do roadwork in the snow, it makes you sick," Ali countered.

Once, Muhammad reflected on a $100,000 fee he received for attending two promotional screenings of a made-for-television documentary and told me, "Ain't life amazing. Twenty-five years ago, they wouldn't let me fight to earn a living. And now they're paying me $100,000 to go to the movies."

Another time, Ali stopped to shake hands with an elderly white man who had a deep Southern accent.

"How old are you?" Muhammad queried.

"Eighty-one."

"Where are you from?"

"Mississippi."

"Did you ever call anyone a nigger?"

"Oh, no. Not me."

After the man left, Muhammad turned to me, laughing. "Do you believe that? An eighty-one-year-old white man from Mississippi; never called anyone a nigger."

Shortly thereafter, we attended a tribute to Muhammad at the Smithsonian Institution in Washington, D.C. I made some opening remarks and referred to an incident that had occurred years earlier when Ali took a shuttle flight from Washington to New York. As the flight crew readied for take-off, an attendant instructed, "Mr. Ali, please buckle your seatbelt."

"Superman don't need no seatbelt," Ali informed her.

"Mr. Ali," the flight attendant said sweetly. "Superman don't need no plane."

When I retold that story, Muhammad's face lit up and he laughed as hard as anyone in the audience. Ali's ability to laugh at himself also surfaced when we authorized Easton Press to publish 3,500 copies of a leather-bound edition of *Muhammad Ali: His Life and Times*. Pursuant to contract, we each agreed to sign 3,500 signature pages for insertion in the book. I was to receive three dollars per signature; Ali, considerably more.

"This is fantastic," I told myself. "If I do ten signatures a minute, that's 600 signatures an hour . . . Divide 3,500 by 600 . . . Wow! I'll get $10,500 for six hours work."

Except when I started signing, I found that I couldn't sign more than a few hundred pages at a time. "Any more than that," I confided in Muhammad, "and I can't connect the letters properly. Something starts misfiring in my brain."

"Now you know," Ali told me, referring to his own physical condition. "It wasn't boxing. It was the autographs."

Our spending time together also rekindled memories for Muhammad. In 1996, we were on a media bus in Atlanta. Several video monitors were showing a tape of Cassius Clay's antics prior to his first fight against Sonny Liston.

"It's sad Sonny Liston is dead," Muhammad told me. "I'd like to be able to sit down with him. Two old men, just sitting around, talking about old times."

"What would you say to him?"

Ali's eyes grew wide. "I'd tell him, 'Man, you scared me.'"

Then "The Rumble in the Jungle" came on the screen, and Ali's eyes grew wistful.

"So many people come up to me and tell me they remember where they were when I whupped George Foreman. I remember where I was too."

"What were you thinking when you looked down at Foreman on the canvas?"

"It felt good."

"But what was going through your mind?" I pressed.

"I didn't think. Things just happened."

The perfect metaphor for Ali's life, if ever there was one.

That same year, Muhammad and I traveled around the United States to speak with students about the need for tolerance and understanding. One person who was particularly supportive of our efforts was Roy Jones, who attended several gatherings with us including one at Locke High School in Los Angeles.

When Muhammad was introduced in Los Angeles, he received his usual roar of acclamation. But Roy got something extra. When his name was mentioned, a substantial number of the girls screamed the kind of scream reserved over the decades for Elvis Presley, the Beatles, and other heartthrobs. And Muhammad didn't miss a beat. Feigning jealousy, he stood up from his chair, smacked his fist into the palm of his hand, and challenged Roy to fight. Roy responded. And for thirty seconds, two of the greatest fighters of all time sparred for an adoring crowd.

Muhammad and Roy were having fun. But as fighters, they were also measuring each other.

"He's good," Muhammad said afterward. "He has good moves, and he's fast."

"I was surprised at how well Ali moved," Roy acknowledged. "He's got a lot more left than most people realize."

But as usual, Muhammad had the last word. "Take my advice," he told Roy when it was over. "Get a gun."

I also remember the year that Muhammad telephoned to wish me a Merry Christmas. "Think about it," I suggested. "A Muslim calling a Jew to wish him well on a Christian holiday. There's a message in that for anyone who's listening."

"We're all trying to get to the same place," Muhammad told me. And the Ali magic remains. It always will. A while back, Muhammad was at a party, surrounded by the usual chaos that accompanies his presence. Men who would rarely think of hugging another man fell into his embrace. Women were asking for kisses. There were requests for autographs and photographs when, amidst it all, a mother brought her four-year-old daughter over to Ali.

"Do you know who this is?" she asked her child.

The four-year-old nodded reverentially and told her mother, "It's the Easter Bunny."

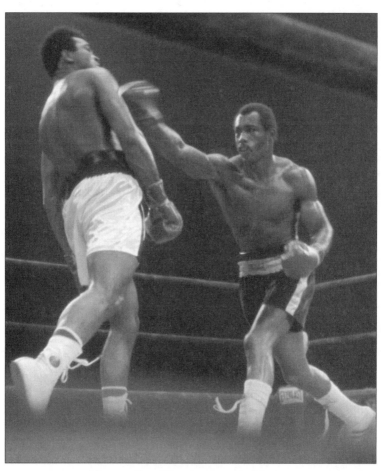

Ali evades Ken Norton's blows.

"I'm Coming Back To Whup Mike Tyson's Butt"
(1988)

Author's Note: This is the piece (referenced at page 88) that I wrote for Ali prior to our meeting in October 1988. Muhammad had respect for Mike Tyson as a fighter, but considered him beatable. It was his view that Iron Mike would have knocked out Joe Frazier, but that George Foreman would have kayoed Tyson. Even when Mike was undefeated, Ali told me, "Tyson is predictable, the way he moves his head. He has fast hands, but he's slow on his feet and my hands were faster than his. The way to beat Tyson is with a fast jab, a hard right hand; and if he hits you, you have to be able to take a punch."

Still, many commentators saw things differently. And I sensed that Muhammad was a bit miffed by the view that Iron Mike would have beaten him. Thus, I wasn't surprised when my telephone rang on the night of February 11, 1990, moments after James "Buster" Douglas dethroned Mike Tyson in Tokyo. "What do you think people will say now when someone asks them, who was greater, Mike Tyson or me?" Muhammad asked rhetorically. "Buster Douglas saved me the trouble of coming back and whupping Mike Tyson myself."

People are weeping and crying all the time these days, because Mike Tyson is heavyweight champion of the world. He's a bully, and no one can beat him. But that don't mean nuthin'. They said Sonny Liston was unbeatable, and I beat him. They said George Foreman was unbeatable, and I beat him. They say Tyson is unbeatable, but I'm coming back. I got a time machine, and I'm coming back to whup Mike Tyson.

Mike Tyson is too ugly to be champion. He's got gold teeth. He's got bald spots all over his head. I used to call Joe Frazier "The Gorilla," but next to Tyson, Joe Frazier was like a beautiful woman. Everyone I fought, I had names for. Sonny Liston was "The Bear." George Chuvalo was "The Washer Woman." Floyd Patterson was "The Rabbit." George Foreman was "The Mummy." Mike Tyson is ugly; he's ugly like King Kong, so I'm calling him "Kong."

And Tyson is nuthin'. He never fought no one. He fought Larry Holmes when Holmes was an old man. He fought Trevor Berbick, and Berbick was a crazy old man. He fought Tyrell Biggs, and Biggs was an amateur. Michael Spinks was a light-heavyweight. Tony Tubbs, he was an embarrassment. Bonecrusher Smith, he lost the first nine rounds against Frank Bruno. Tyson never fought Sonny Liston, he never fought Joe Frazier, he never fought George Foreman like I did, fighting all of them in their prime.

So I'm coming back to whup Mike Tyson. It's the biggest fight in the history of time. Bigger than David against Goliath; bigger than Napoleon against England and Russia. Too big for home television. Too big for closed circuit. They're putting this fight on special 3-D closed-circuit with cameras and lenses like you ain't never seen before.

And the whole world is holding its breath. Everyone's rooting for me, but they're saying, Muhammad Ali, he's just a man and now he's fighting Kong. They're saying Mike Tyson is too strong, too mean. He hits too hard.

Here's how it goes.

Round One: It'll be all over in one; that's what they're saying. And Tyson comes out for the kill. Ali's dancing, jabbing. Pop-pop-pop-pop. Tyson swings—WHOOSH—hits nuthin' but air.

Pop-pop-pop-pop.

WHOOSH. Tyson hits nuthin' but air again.

Pop-pop-pop-pop. At the end of the round, the television people are adding up their punch-stats, and they can't believe it. Muhammad Ali: 107 jabs, 92 landed. Mike Tyson: 40 punches, and

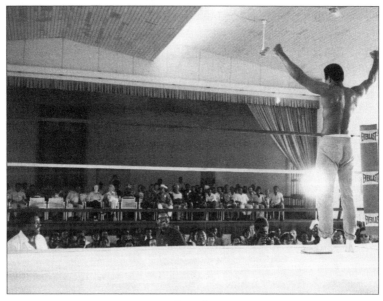

Posing for the press.

he didn't land one.

Round Two: It's just like round one.

Pop-pop-pop-pop.

WHOOSH.

Pop-pop-pop-pop.

WHOOSH.

Ali is pretty. The crowd's going wild. *Ali! Ali!*

Tyson lands a punch, but it don't do no harm.

Round Three: Ali's landing right hands. It's early in the fight, and already Tyson's left eye is starting to close. Women and children are holding their breath. Ali looks good. He's better than good. Muhammad Ali is the greatest, but there's nine more rounds to go, and Tyson is getting dirty now. He's butting and thumbing, throwing elbows and hitting low.

Round Four: Pop-pop-pop-pop. Ali is still dancing. Floats like a butterfly, but he stings like a bee. Pop-pop-pop-pop. Tyson is bleeding; the left eye. He's cut and the blood is flowing down. The experts are shaking their heads. Muhammad Ali is making Tyson look like a child.

Round Five: Tyson is taking a bad whuppin'. The crowd's going wild. Ali! Ali! Tyson's getting tired. Ali's talking to him, asking, "Who's the greatest?" Tyson won't answer, so Ali hits him four-five-six right hands.

Round Six: It's the Ali Shuffle. Two billion people 'round the world, they're jumping up and down, hugging each other, weeping with joy. It's the real Ali. Not the Ali who lost to Larry Holmes; not the Ali you thought was old. This is Muhammad Ali, who destroyed Zora Folley; Muhammad Ali, who done in Cleveland Williams. Ali! Ali!

Round Seven: Tyson's gold teeth get knocked out into the crowd, and you can see his mother-in-law running after them. The crowd's in a state of histomania. Ali's punching so fast now, no one can hear the pops. It's p-p-p-p-p-p-p-p. Ali winds up for a bolo punch. The crowd is praying. They're pleading, don't take no chances; don't get careless with Tyson. But Ali's still winding up for the bolo, and Tyson's moving closer. Tyson is getting ready. He's gonna kill Ali. The crowd holds its breath. Tyson leaps with a left hook. But Muhammad Ali throws a right hand. It's faster than a speeding bullet. Faster than the punch that knocked down Sonny Liston. The eye can't see it, except with a super slo-mo replay camera.

TYSON IS DOWN ! ! !

Tyson gets up at seven.

Ding! There's the bell.

And now Tyson is mad. He's embarrassed. He's been humiliated. He's coming out for the next round, determined to put Muhammad Ali down.

Round Eight: Tyson charges out of his corner, throwing punches like wild. He's spitting blood. There's fire in his eyes. He's doing everything he can. And . . . OH NO ! Ali is tired. Ali has stopped dancing. After seven rounds with Kong, Ali's legs are gone. Ali's moving back. Tyson comes in for the kill. Ali's in a corner; he's in trouble. Tyson is ugly. He's a monster that has to be fed, and Muhammad Ali is the monster's meal.

Tyson with a left. Tyson with a right. The whole world is covering its eyes.

Wait a minute ! ! !

IT'S THE ROPE-A-DOPE ! ! !

Muhammad Ali tricked the monster, and now Ali is coming back strong.

Ali with a left. Ali with a right. It's Muhammad Ali, the greatest fighter of all time.

AND TYSON IS DOWN ! ! !

The count is one, two . . .

Tyson's eyes are closed!

Three, four . . .

He's not moving!

Five, six . . .

We have a brand new champion!

Seven, eight . . .

This is the greatest moment of all time!

Nine, ten . . .

It's all over! It's all over! The tyrant is dead! Long live the true King!

Jim Brown and Muhammad Ali.

Ali at Notre Dame:
A Night To Remember
(1998)

Notre Dame versus Michigan, 1990. The first game of the season for two of college football's most fabled institutions. Notre Dame was the top-ranked team in the country. Michigan was rated as high as number two, depending on which poll you followed. The game had been sold out for months and was the hottest ticket in the nation.

Meanwhile, Howard Bingham and I were tired. Howard is Muhammad Ali's best friend. I was Ali's biographer. It was the day before the game, and we'd been reading aloud for five days. More specifically, we'd been reading the manuscript for *Muhammad Ali: His Life and Times*—all one thousand pages—with Muhammad and his wife Lonnie. I'd just finished the first draft of the book and wanted to make sure it was factually accurate. Also, I knew that reading it aloud would be the best way to elicit further thoughts from Muhammad.

Howard and I are sports fans. And since Notre Dame is only a twenty-minute drive from the Ali's home, we thought it would be fun to go to the game. Ali doesn't care a whole lot about football. But his presence opens doors; he likes big events, and he's a sweetheart when it comes to doing things for friends. Thus, my call to the Notre Dame Athletic Department: "Would it be possible for Muhammad Ali to buy three tickets for tomorrow night's game?"

There was a long pause on the other end of the line. "Let me call you back," the woman said. Five minutes later, the telephone rang. "How do we know the tickets are really for Mr. Ali?"

"That's easy," I told her. "He'll pick them up in person."

"All right, come by the Athletic Department today before five o'clock."

"Do you want Muhammad to bring his driver's license for identification?"

"That's not necessary. I think we'll recognize him."

Shortly before noon, we drove to Notre Dame to pick up the tickets. The Athletic Department wanted to give them to us, but we insisted on paying; a small gesture given their open-market value. Then we went home, read *Muhammad Ali: His Life and Times* for another five hours, read some more on Saturday, and drove back to Notre Dame.

The game was scheduled for 8:00 p.m. Central Standard Time. We arrived around six o'clock. The weather was perfect, and the scene surrounding the stadium was quintessential bigtime college football. Tens of thousands of fans had set up grills and were barbecuing everything from hamburgers to shrimp. Many of them didn't even have tickets to the game. They just wanted to be near the action, and their reaction to Muhammad was as expected. As we walked around, we heard a lot of "Omigod! It's Muhammad Ali." And Muhammad has certain opportunities that aren't available to the rest of us. For example, he can walk around a tailgate party until he finds something that looks particularly good to eat, and what he invariably hears is, "Muhammad Ali! Please join us."

In other words, we ate quite well thanks to the generosity of strangers. Then we went inside the stadium to our seats, which happened to be on the fifty yard line. That was nice for us; and I suspect, also good for Notre Dame recruiting since the folks around us were suitably impressed by Ali's presence.

Muhammad sat between Howard and myself. Notre Dame was coached by Lou Holtz. Its brightest star was Raghib Ismail, who was joined in the backfield by Rick Mirer, Tony Brooks, Ricky Watters, and Rodney Culverhouse. Michigan was in its first year under new head coach Gary Moeller, who had the unenviable task of succeeding Bo Schembechler. But his job was made easier by the presence of Elvis Grbac, Jarrod Bunch, Jon Vaughn, and Greg Skrepenak.

It was a great game. Notre Dame surged to a 14-3 lead, and it seemed as though everyone on earth was singing, "Cheer, cheer for old Notre Dame." Then Michigan began to roll and scored three unanswered touchdowns, whereupon *Hail to the Victors Valiant* was very much in vogue.

Meanwhile, as the game progressed, I began to talk with an elderly woman sitting to my left. She was Ellen Stonebreaker, grandmother of the Notre Dame co-captain and middle-linebacker, Mike Stonebreaker. If I had to guess, I'd say she was about eighty. She was charming. And when Notre Dame was on defense, her eyes never left the field. Even Ali noticed the intensity with which she was watching. "Look at that old lady," he told me. "She's like a hawk."

Notre Dame won. Down ten points going into the fourth quarter, they rallied for two late touchdowns capped by an 18-yard scoring pass from Mirer to Adrian Jarrell with 1:40 left to play. But one moment stands out in my mind.

It came in the second half. Ellen Stonebreaker had been sneaking glances at Muhammad for some time. Finally she said to me, "You know something; that boxer is a good looking fellow."

"Tell her I don't fool around with white women," Muhammad advised me. Which I duly reported to Mrs. Stonebreaker, who seemed more bemused than disappointed. However, she did have one request.

"I haven't done this since I was a young girl," she acknowledged. "But could you get me that fellow's autograph."

I asked how she'd like her name written. She said she'd prefer it if Muhammad used her maiden name. She spelled it for him. He wrote it out, drew a little heart, and signed "Love, Muhammad Ali."

Then he kissed her.

It was just another day for Muhammad; one that I'm sure he's long since forgotten. But as is often the case, whenever and wherever he travels, it was a memorable night for everyone around him.

A *SPORT* photo shoot with Ali's children in 1974.

Muhammad Ali: Thanksgiving 1996
(1996)

As is his custom, Muhammad Ali awoke shortly after 5:00 a.m. on Thanksgiving Day 1996. He was in Los Angeles to pursue his latest mission, teaching people how to love. *HEALING* is a cause that Ali can wrap himself around.

After washing himself with clear running water, Ali put on clean clothes and said the first of his five daily prayers. Then he moved behind his hotel-room desk and began signing bookplates that would be distributed to fans who attended one of several book-signings in the days ahead. Ali's weight has been over 250 pounds for several years, and now he's decided to get down to 220. Accordingly, he skipped breakfast as part of his personalized brand of dieting and announced, "This is my third day of not eating, except for one meal a day," However, as the day progressed, Ali ate pears, apples, and oranges from a large basket of fruit that had been sent to his room by the hotel management.

"And maybe a muffin," Ali admitted.

Correct that. Several muffins. And chocolate chip cookies, cheese, and crackers; all before his "one meal of the day"—a large Thanksgiving dinner.

"I'm losing weight because I'm planning a comeback," Ali said. "On my fifty-fifth birthday, I think I'll fight the top three heavyweights in the world, one round each, at Madison Square Garden."

"You'd better get in shape fast," Muhammad was cautioned. "Your fifty-fifth birthday is in seven weeks."

"Seven weeks? Maybe I'll do it when I'm sixty instead."

At 9:00 a.m. Pacific Coast time, Ali turned on the television to accommodate a guest who wanted to watch the Kansas City Chiefs versus the Detroit Lions. "In my whole life," he admitted, "I've never watched a football game on television from beginning to end. Sometimes I go to the Super Bowl because the people around me want to go, and because of me, they can get in. But the only sports I'm interested in now are big fights. I like watching big fights to see how I'd do if I was in them."

The Detroit Lions scored a touchdown, and the obligatory end zone dance followed.

"You started that," Ali was told. "All the dancing and celebrating and showing off started with you."

"I started the big salaries too. Big salaries started when me and Joe Frazier got $2,500,000 each the first time we fought."

The Chiefs vanquished the Lions 28-24, at which point the Dallas Cowboys took the field against the Washington Redskins. Meanwhile, Ali had begun turning the pages of a Bible, pointing out contradictions.

"Look at Exodus 33:11 [And the Lord spake unto Moses face to face, as a man speaketh unto his friend]. Now look at Exodus 33:20 [And the Lord said, 'Thou canst not see my face, for there shall be no man see me and live']. Some people think the Bible is the word of God," Ali continued. "But in one part of Exodus, it says Moses saw God's face. And in another part, it says no man can see God and live. How can the word of God be two different things? Here's another contradiction. John 5:31 [Jesus said, 'If I bear witness of myself, my witness is not true']. Now read John 8:14 [Jesus answered and said unto them, 'Though I bear record of myself, yet my record is true']. You're educated. You tell me, is Jesus' witness true or not true? Heavy, ain't it?"

Shortly after 2:00 p.m., Ali left the hotel to travel to the home of Connye Richardson, a longtime family friend. Richardson lives in Hancock Park, the section of Los Angeles that Ali lived in during his marriage to Veronica Porche. Ali has mixed feelings about his years in Los Angeles. The period encompassed some of his greatest glories, but it was in Hancock Park that his fortunes began to turn. He was living there when he lost to Leon Spinks, Larry Holmes and Trevor Berbick. It was in Hancock Park that his health began to fail, his family life [now on solid foundation again] began to unravel, and he felt himself growing old.

Connye Richardson's home was spacious and comfortable. During the course of the day, twenty family members and friends dropped by. Ali was wearing tan slacks and a white short-sleeved shirt, his still-powerful forearms visible. Thanks to new medication [a combination of Artane and Medapar] his voice was clearer and his face more animated than they have been for several years.

As he often does when he feels at home in someone else's living room, Muhammad turned on the television. A movie about Vietnam starring Gene Hackman was showing. The last twenty minutes were unremitting violence and gore. "I made a wise decision when I didn't go to Vietnam," Ali told one of the other guests. "All that killing was wrong." Then he switched to CNN, which had a brief feature on a presidential pardon given by Bill Clinton to a forty-five pound turkey. Instead of winding up on someone's dinner table, the turkey would spend the rest of its years on a petting farm in Virginia. Ali was asked if he thinks it's right for people to kill animals to eat when other types of food are available. He considered the issue and responded, "Everything that God made, he made for a purpose. I don't believe in hunting just to kill an animal. That bothers me. But I think it's all right to eat animals like turkeys and fish and cows."

Connye Richardson had been cooking for days, and it seemed as though every one of God's foods was served. If Muhammad is truly planning to fight again in Madison Square Garden, this wasn't the place to slim down. But it was a good Thanksgiving. And Ali was both happy and in a reflective mood as the day drew to a close.

"God has been good to me," Muhammad said in the car going back to the hotel. "I'm thankful I've got a good wife and nine healthy children. I'm thankful I was three-time heavyweight champion of the world. I'm thankful I live in a country like America. I'm thankful I've been able to travel and meet people all over the world. I'm thankful that, even though I haven't fought for fifteen years, people still remember me. I have a good life."

Ali and Sugar Ray Robinson.

Pensacola, Florida: February 27, 1997

As noted earlier in this volume, I spent part of 1996 and 1997 traveling around the country with Muhammad Ali, speaking to students about tolerance and understanding. On February 27, 1997, our travels took us to Pensacola, Florida. The plan called for Muhammad and myself to address 7,600 students at the Pensacola Civic Center on the subject of HEALING. But a group of Christian fundamentalists threatened legal action to halt the event, claiming that our appearance was a plot between a Muslim and a Jew to teach heresy to their children. For several weeks, a controversy raged. Then, inexorably, the community came together in support of our visit. Florida Governor Lawton Chiles attended the assembly and praised its purpose. The event was an enormous success. My own remarks to the students of Pensacola follow.

As most of you know, Muhammad Ali and I have co-authored a book about bigotry and prejudice. Early in the book, there's a statement by Muhammad that has led to some controversy in Pensacola, and I'd like to discuss that quotation with you. Muhammad's words were as follows:

My mother was a Baptist. She believed Jesus was the son of God, and I don't believe that. But even though my mother had a religion different from me, I believe that on Judgment Day my mother will be in Heaven. There are Jewish people who lead good lives; and when they die, I believe they're going to heaven. If you're a good Muslim, if you're a good Christian, if you're a good Jew; it doesn't matter what religion you are. If you're a good person, you'll receive God's blessing.

The words I just read to you reflect Muhammad's belief that all people serve the same God; we just serve Him in different ways. Obviously, there are people who disagree with Muhammad's view. They believe that the only way a person can go to Heaven is to embrace Jesus Christ as his, or her, Savior. That belief is their right. But some people in this community have carried their beliefs a step further by trying to halt this assembly.

I got a telephone call recently from one of these people. She didn't give her name. Instead, she began by demanding, "How dare you question the word of God?" I told her, "I'm not questioning the word of God. I'm questioning your ability to interpret the word of God for me, because I believe in a loving God, who bestows His blessings upon all people." And that was the end of the conversation, because she hung up.

Now, I want to make it as clear as I possibly can that no one on this stage today is here to challenge what any of you believe insofar as it relates to your own personal religious convictions. I hope you like your religion and are fully satisfied with it. Muhammad and I like our respective religions too. All we ask is that you keep in mind that we all have the same Creator, and all of us have to work to get along. Our message is simple. Let's understand each other and be tolerant of our differences, whether those differences relate to our religion, the color of our skin, the language we speak, the country we come from, or any of the other sources of diversity that sometimes divide us.

As you go through life, you will find that your education, your jobs, your personal relationships, and your government, are all dependent in varying degree upon the will of others. That's the nature of living. No one goes through this world on their own. But there's one area where each of you will have total control over your own destiny. Each and every one of you has complete control over your own moral fiber. That means you can be as bigoted and prejudiced and hateful—or as tolerant and understanding—as you want to be. Hate is ugly. It's ugly when it's shouted out on the street. And it's ugly—it will eat you up and destroy you—when it lies in your heart. So if you hate, let go of it.

It's unlikely that any of you will ever become as good a fighter as Muhammad Ali, or have the same impact on history as Muhammad Ali. But in your own way, each of you can become as good a person as Muhammad Ali. All you have to do is take the best qualities that people like Muhammad have to offer and make them part of your own individual personalities. But don't stop with famous people. There's a horrible misconception in our society that just because someone is famous or a big celebrity that that person is a hero or a good role model. And that's not necessarily the case. Some celebrities are lousy role models.

But if you look around, you'll find people in your everyday lives who are wonderful role models. I'm sure there are teachers in your schools who care about you and work hard to give you the best education they possibly can. Those teachers are wonderful role models. I would hope that all of you have one or more relatives who love you and provide for you and do everything they can to give you good values. Those relatives are wonderful role models. And whether you know it or not, each of you is a role model. There are kids in grade school who look up to you and want to be like you. Many of you have younger brothers and sisters who feel the same way. And as role models, you young men and women have a responsibility to be the best people you can possibly be.

Focus on what's best in yourselves. Learn to treat other people with dignity and respect. Learn how to love.

Thank you.

A Day of Remembrance
(1997)

On June 24, 1997, Muhammad Ali awoke in the nation's capitol at 5:00 a.m. He said his prayers, ate a light breakfast, and read quietly from the Qur'an. Then, accompanied by his wife Lonnie and several friends, he left the Hay-Adams Hotel and drove to a unique destination—the United States Holocaust Memorial Museum.

The museum was not yet open to the public when Ali arrived at 7:45 a.m. He had come early because he feared his presence during normal visiting hours would cause a commotion unsuited to the decorum of his surroundings. Several staff members greeted Muhammad and his party when they arrived. There were introductions, and the tour began.

The mission of the United States Holocaust Memorial Museum is to inform, honor, and inspire. More specifically, it is designed to present the history of the persecution and murder of six million Jews and millions of other victims of Nazi tyranny; to commemorate those who died; and to encourage visitors to contemplate the moral implications of their own civic responsibilities.

Ali began by assimilating facts as he walked through the museum . . . One-and-a-half million children were exterminated in The Holocaust . . . It wasn't just Jews . . . Gypsies, the physically disabled, mentally handicapped, and other "undesirables" were also victims . . . Books were burned, synagogues destroyed . . .

As the tour progressed, Muhammad began to draw parallels

between The Holocaust and the slavery that his own ancestors endured. Ali has spoken often about how black Americans were robbed of their African names and given slave names instead. Now he learned of people whose Jewish names were replaced by numbers tattooed on their forearms. Standing in a boxcar used to transport Jews to death camps in Poland, he imagined himself in the cargo hold of a slaveship two centuries earlier.

Midway through the tour, Ali came to a glass wall bearing the names of thousands of communities eradicated during The Holocaust.

"Each of these names is a whole town?" Muhammad asked incredulously.

"Yes."

"I never knew it was that bad."

The tour went on . . . A pile of shoes taken from the dead at Majdanek . . . Bales of hair cut from the heads of concentration camp victims . . . A crude metal table where bodies were placed and gold teeth extracted with pliers . . . Grainy films of nude bodies piled high being bulldozed into trenches.

Ninety minutes after the tour began, Ali stopped to read a quotation in silver letters on a gray wall:

First they came for the socialists.
And I did not speak out because I was not a socialist.
Then they came for the trade unionists.
And I did not speak out because I was not a trade unionist.
Then they came for the Jews.
And I did not speak out because I was not a Jew.
Then they came for me.
And there was no one left to speak for me.

Finally, Ali entered the Hall of Remembrance and placed a white rose beside the museum's eternal flame.

During the course of his life, Muhammad Ali has taken many courageous stands. But his presence at the United States Holocaust Memorial Museum on June 24, 1997, is among his most important statements of principle.

The victims' faces on this particular morning were Jewish. But they could just as easily have been faces from Cambodia, Bosnia, or Rwanda. By virtue of his presence, Ali demonstrated once again his solidarity with all victims of persecution. And he joined his spirit with millions of Holocaust victims and with the survivors who remember them.

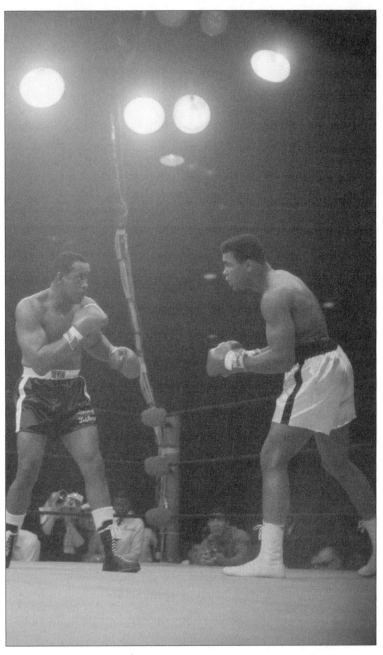

Liston vs. Ali in Lewiston, Maine in 1965.

"Did Barbra Streisand Whup Sonny Liston?"
(1996)

On February 7, 1996, I was in the lobby of the ANA-Westin Hotel in Washington, D.C., with Muhammad Ali, Jim Brown, Ralph Boston, and a handful of others. That night, HBO would present a promotional screening of *The Journey of the African-American Athlete*. In anticipation of the event, ten people had been invited to the White House to meet with President Clinton in the Oval Office. My name was on the list, along with Nancy Bronson, whom I'd been dating for six months. The mini-bus that would take us to the White House was pulling up to the hotel when Seth Abraham (President of Time Warner Sports) approached me with a look of consternation.

"Didn't anybody tell you?"

"Tell me what?"

"Yesterday, the White House took you and Nancy off the guest list. You've been replaced by Zina Garrison and Calvin Hill."

Seth was apologetic.

Nancy was accepting.

And Muhammad was . . . Well, Muhammad was Muhammad.

"Stay by me. I'll get you into the White House."

"Don't waste your time," Paul Costello (Time Warner's point man in Washington) told us. "No one just walks into the Oval Office. In fact, no one gets past the White House gate without advance security clearance. All that will happen is, you'll have to turn around and take a cab back to the hotel."

Which seemed likely. But Nancy and I had nothing to lose, so we boarded the mini-bus with the others. When we arrived at the first security checkpoint by a wrought-iron gate outside the White House, a guard asked for ID's from everybody. Five minutes passed. Several limousines drove by. Then the guard returned.

"There's two people who don't have security clearance. Who are Hauser and Bronson?"

Nancy and I raised our hands.

"Come with me, please."

Nancy and I got off the mini-bus and followed the guard to the security booth where I pleaded our cause. "I was told on Monday that we'd been approved by the White House . . . No one told us our names had been taken off the list . . ."

The guard was polite but unyielding. "I'm sorry, you can't go any further."

At which point, Muhammad joined us.

The guard repeated what he'd just said. "Mr. Ali, this man and this woman don't have security clearance. I'm sure you understand how these things work. They simply can't go any further."

And Muhammad was understanding—"If they don't go, I ain't going."

Unsure as to what to do next, the guard telephoned the White House. Minutes later, an official-looking man with a mustache strode down to the gate to meet us.

"What seems to be the problem?" Obviously, he already knew what they problem was, because before I could answer, we were advised, "Look, this is my event. Your names aren't on the list, and that's the end of it. No one without security clearance is allowed past this gate."

"But these are my friends."

"Mr. Ali, you don't understand."

Nancy got back on the mini-bus, and Paul Costello came over to monitor the proceedings. There followed an explanation about how Barbra Streisand had recently been invited to the White House. *The* Barbra Streisand, who had helped raise millions of dollars for the Democratic party and was a personal friend of the President and

Mrs. Clinton. Yet when Ms. Streisand brought someone with her for her appointment with the President, her friend was turned away at the gate.

And Muhammad was duly impressed.

"Did Barbra Streisand whup Joe Frazier?"

"Mr. Ali—"

"Did Barbra Streisand whup Sonny Liston?"

The Man With The Mustache, who I'm sure is a fine public servant and was just trying to do his job, excused himself and returned moments later. "All right, we've got to get this show on the road, so you two [pointing to Nancy and me] can go as far as the reception area, but that's all."

The mini-bus proceeded to the West Wing of the White House, where we were ushered into a reception area. There was small talk. Several minutes passed. Then The Man With The Mustache reappeared. "Those of you with security clearance, come with me into the Roosevelt Room. You two [pointing to Nancy and me], stay here."

The members of the group with security clearance were ushered into the Roosevelt Room, directly across the corridor from the Oval Office. Nancy and I stayed in the reception area, settling on a sofa. Inside the Roosevelt Room, various cabinet members, presidential aides, and White House staffers had gathered for a "photo op" with Muhammad.

Except Muhammad wasn't there. He was with Nancy and me in the reception area beneath a painting of "George Washington Crossing the Delaware."

Which is how Nancy and I got into the Roosevelt Room.

"But I'm telling you now," The Man With The Mustache warned. "You are not going into the Oval Office, and I mean it."

And he did mean it.

When the time came to enter the President's office, The Man With The Mustache approached. "You two [Nancy and me], sit over there [pointing to the far side of the conference table]."

He waited until we'd followed his command.

"Now, I'd like the rest of you to line up over here."

At which point, I said to Nancy, "Look, there's no way that both of us will make it into the Oval Office. When the others go in, just walk over to Muhammad and take his arm."

"What about you?"

"I'll stay here."

"That's not fair to you."

"Sure, it is. I've been to the White House. I already have a photo of me with the President."

"Not in the Oval Office."

"It doesn't matter. You can go into the office for both of us."

Across the corridor, the door to the Oval Office opened. We saw the President of the United States standing there.

The line started to move forward.

Nancy got up from the sofa, walked over to Muhammad, and with considerable trepidation took his arm—

The Man With The Mustache walked over to Nancy, and stood in front of her. "Mr. Ali," he importuned. "The President of the United States is waiting for you."

And Muhammad walked forward, alone.

Nancy and I watched from a distance as the President greeted his guests. Then the door to the Oval Office closed, and we were left in the Roosevelt Room.

I was disappointed. I won't tell you I wasn't. For a while, we explored our surroundings, which was kind of fun. If you're ever in the Roosevelt Room, I suggest you look at the gold medallion given to Teddy Roosevelt in 1906 when he won the Nobel Peace Prize. Also, check out the bronze sculpture by Alexander Pope, and the portraits of Teddy, Franklin, and Eleanor Roosevelt.

Nancy did her best to put a good face on things. "Tom, this is really very exciting. We're having a wonderful time in Washington with Muhammad. We're in the White House. We saw the President from a few yards away. Don't feel bad for me."

But I did feel bad, for both of us.

Muhammad and the others stayed in the Oval Office for about ten minutes. Then the door to the President's office opened, and they filed out, moving down an adjacent corridor.

Jim Brown . . . Ralph Boston . . . Calvin Hill . . . Zina Garrison . . .

All but one.

Finally, Muhammad Ali walked out of the Oval Office—leading the President of the United States by the arm toward the Roosevelt Room.

"These are my friends," Muhammad told him.

Bill Clinton smiled, and beckoned us forward with a wave of his arm toward the Oval Office.

"Come on in."

The minutes that followed will remain forever etched in my mind. The President began by asking Nancy her name. Then he turned to me. We chatted briefly; the President was warm and gracious. Eventually, he even called in a photographer. But what I remember most about that afternoon, and always will, is something I've seen many times, something that has been on display for the entire world for almost four decades—the sweetness, the determination, the power, and the magic of Muhammad Ali.

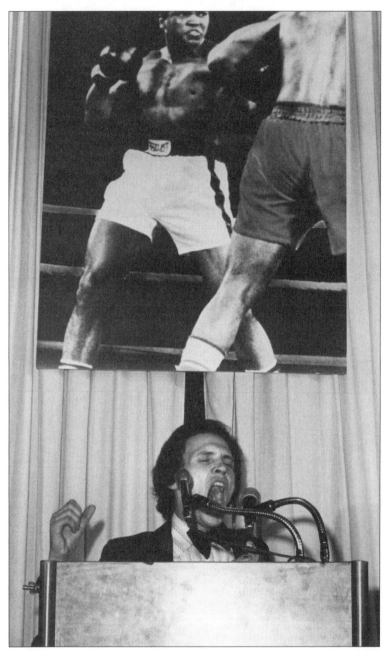

Billy Crystal becomes "The Greatest."

A LIFE IN QUOTES

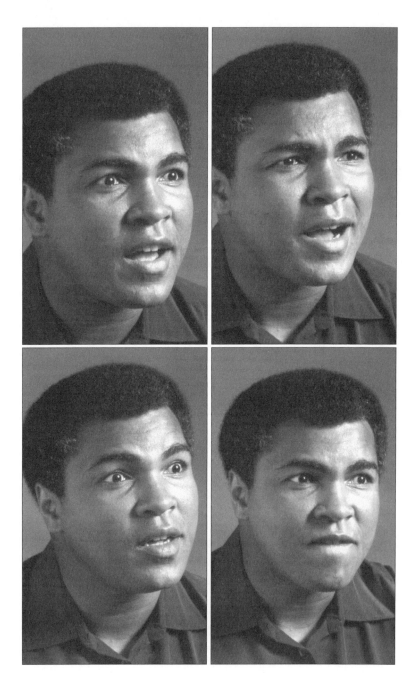

A Life in Quotes

In his prime, Muhammad Ali was one of the most verbally gifted athletes in the history of sports.

The following pages offer a sampler of quotes and anecdotal recollections from and about Ali. As with the rest of this book, an effort has been made to avoid duplicating material contained in Muhammad Ali: His Life and Times. *Thus, the quotes aren't intended to be all-inclusive. Rather, they're designed to show Ali's essence, the sweep of his career, and his impact on people.*

Jim Bell [a childhood classmate of Cassius Clay]: We were in elementary school together, and he was just another one of the kids. You push and you shove each other, and get into the normal fights. There were days he lost, and there were days he won. So when he beat Sonny Liston to win the championship, some of us were laughing about it, saying, "He's not even undefeated in the neighborhood. How can he be champion of the world?"

Ronnie O'Keefe [Cassius Clay's opponent in his first amateur fight. It was the only fight of O'Keefe's ring career]: I weighed 89 pounds, and he weighed about the same. The fight was three rounds, a minute a round. And he hit me a whole lot more than I hit him. I had a heck of a headache that night. He won by a split decision. And right after he was announced the winner by the referee, he started shouting that he was going to be the greatest fighter ever. He was heavyweight champion of the world already, at twelve years old and 89 pounds.

Joe Martin [the Louisville policeman who taught 12-year-old Cassius Clay how to box]: He's been popping off before fights from the very beginning, and it's not a thing in the world but whistling past the graveyard. He's just overcoming the fear that's in him.

Sister James Ellen Huff [who supervised Cassius Clay's first regular after-school job]: He was a sophomore in high school. Somebody had to dust up the library. And a schoolmate, who had been doing the job and was going to leave, brought him over. He was already known. Unknown to me, but he was appearing in Golden Gloves tournaments at the time, and had a whole bag of trophies that he brought out to show me later when I found out that he was a boxing champion. His friend introduced him to me as Cassius Clay. I said, "Do they call you Cass?" And he told me, "No ma'am; Cassius Marcellus Clay, Junior." So I said, "Okay, it will be Cassius." And he was polite; he was gentle. He always appeared on time and related to his work beautifully. Except one time. His father was a painter. And Cassius was kind of given to art too, so I gave him a paint job down in the lower area where we were working. And he resisted. He used enamel where I had asked him to use flat paint. I said, "I thought your father was a painter." And he told me that his father was an artist, not a barn painter. And he just lived boxing. He worked at it very hard. One evening—he'd been training pretty heavily I think—I came back from dinner. We had some reading tables in the stacks on the second floor. I looked in, and there was Cassius on one of the tables, asleep, facing the wall. I said, "Cassius, are you sick?" He raised himself up, kind of stunned because he'd fallen into a deep sleep, and told me, no. And after he became famous—you read about places where they say, "Abraham Lincoln slept here." Well, I take people into the stacks and I tell them, "Cassius Clay slept here."

Ralph Boston [gold medalist in the long jump at the 1960 Olympic Games]: I'd never heard of this guy. And at age twenty-one, I really wasn't into other sports. I was a track-and-field man, getting ready to go to Rome. I flew into New York, took a bus to the Biltmore Hotel where the Olympic team was staying. And this young guy came up to me, put his hand on my chest, and said, "Ralph Boston! Hold on; I want to take your picture." Then he told me, "You don't know me now, but my name is Cassius Marcellus Clay, Jr." He had this old Brownie Hawkeye camera, where you had to look down to see what you were photographing. And he proceeded to take my picture, along with pictures of just about everyone else he came in contact with during the Olympics. And there's a question I've been asking Ali all my life. "Where is my picture?"

Wilbert "Skeeter" McClure [Cassius Clay's roommate and fellow gold-medal-winner at the 1960 Olympics]: When we were in Rome, we had this place where the athletes would go to dance and listen to music and relax. And Ali didn't dance. That was always interesting to me; how he could float like a butterfly in the ring, but he would not get on the dance floor. The king of moving in the ring, dancing in the ring, didn't dance. And I'll bet he doesn't dance today. I'll bet he still hasn't learned how to dance.

Zbigniew Pietrzykowski [Cassius Clay's opponent in the 1960 Olympic finals]: During the fight itself, I had to work at a very fast pace to avoid his punches. This was good for the first round. Clay was missing a lot of punches. But in the second round, I realized I was losing my strength, and that it would be difficult for me to survive three rounds. I had to think about defense, and that hampered thoughts of victory. It left me with nothing else but to try to survive three rounds and not be knocked out. I would have done anything then to beat him. But later, I began to cherish his victories.

Wilbert "Skeeter" McClure: I was fighting an Italian in Rome for the gold medal, so I figured my chances were not too good. But I went out and beat Carmello Bosce of Italy. I beat him in the last round, and I came back to the dressing room, shouting, "I got it! I got it! I got it!" Eddie Crook had to go out next. Eddie went out, and he came back, shouting "I got it! I got it! I got it!" Eddie was hysterical. He looked like a seven-year-old kid, he was so joyful. And Cassius, he was no nonsense. He was getting ready to go out, concentrating on his objective. Then he went out, got his gold, came back in; and we hugged each other and jumped up and down, and screamed and screamed and screamed. We just couldn't believe it.

Hartmut Scherzer [A German journalist who met Cassius Clay at the Rome Olympics]: He seemed like a nice young man, but we didn't pay that much attention to him. It's not like any of us knew that someday Cassius Clay would become Muhammad Ali.

Dick Schaap [journalist, author, and television commentator]: I went down to Louisville to do a story about him for the *Saturday Evening Post* in late 1960. It was the first major magazine article that was ever done about him, and we spent a lot of time together. Louisville was a Jim Crow city in 1960; so when we went out to eat, we had to go to the black section of town. I was there for four or five days. Every night, we went to the same restaurant. It had an eight-ounce steak and a sixteen-ounce steak on the menu. Every night, he ordered a thirty-two-ounce steak, and every night they gave it to him. Finally, after two or three nights, I asked him, "How do you know they have a thirty-two-ounce steak? It's not on the menu." And he told me, "When I found out you were coming, I went in and told the people here to order them for me." But if there was a moment when I really totally fell in love with this kid, it was when we were driving down the main street in Louisville. We stopped for a traffic light, and there was a very pretty girl standing on the corner. A white girl. I turned to Cassius, which was his name then, and said, "Boy, she's pretty." And he grabbed me, and said, "You're crazy, man. You can get electrocuted for that; a Jew looking at a white girl in Kentucky."

Don Elbaum [matchmaker and boxing promoter]: My first encounter with Ali was when I represented Sonny Banks. His manager was a big car dealer in Detroit; his trainer was Luthor Burgess; and I was an advisor. We looked at films of Clay, and one thing we saw—like everybody else, I might add—was that he had the bad habit of leaning back from punches. So we worked for a month on the idea that, when Clay leaned back, Sonny would take an extra step forward, get on top of him, and throw the hook. Sonny could really whack. And sure enough, round one, Sonny hits him with a left hook and Clay goes down. As time goes by, it's a nice feeling to know that my guy was the first guy to put him down.

Angelo Dundee: Muhammad was always susceptible to the left hook; against Sonny Banks, against Henry Cooper, against Joe Frazier, whoever. You see, no matter how great a fighter is, he always has flaws. And Muhammad's problem was that left hook. He always had a problem evading it.

A. J. Liebling [writing in the *New Yorker* about Cassius Clay being decked by Sonny Banks]: The poet went down.

Michael Katz [sportswriter]: In the early years, you couldn't touch him. The only legitimate criticism—at least people thought it was legitimate—was that he had no chin because he went down against Henry Cooper; he went down against Sonny Banks. We didn't know how good his chin was because, except for the few times he got caught off balance, nobody was hitting him.

Harold Conrad [fight publicist]: I had a gimmick worked out with Ali. It was a magic trick we did together. He'd be someplace with someone, and he'd tell them about a friend of his named Mr. Wizard who had mental telepathy powers. Mr. Wizard was me. Ali would tell this person to pick any card out of a deck of cards, and if they telephoned Mr. Wizard, he'd be able to identify the card they were holding. So they'd pick a card—say, the four of clubs. Then Ali would telephone, and we had this code. As soon as I answered the phone, Ali would say, "Could I speak to Mr. Wizard." I'd go, "Clubs, diamonds, hearts, spades." And when I hit the right suit, Ali would say, "Hello, this is Muhammad." Then I'd start counting. "Two, three, four, five," all the way up to ace. And when I hit the right card, Ali would say, "Mr. Wizard; I've got someone here who doesn't believe in you. I'm gonna put them on the phone, so you can show them how powerful you are." And it worked every time. No one could ever figure out how we did it.

Muhammad Ali [on John F. Kennedy]: I liked him. He tried to do good, and I liked his personality. When he was killed, I felt empty. I got a chill all over. I frightened me that something like that could happen to the president of the entire country right in the center of the country.

Booker Johnson [entourage member]: Malcolm X is the one who really inspired him to become a Muslim. Malcolm was the most eloquent speaker we had among us, and in those days he was telling us something new. He gave us courage, a feeling of independence, and this is what inspired Ali. But Ali had to be taught the religion slowly. You don't just give a baby steak because, if you do, it will choke him.

Dick Schaap: One night—and this goes back to when Ali was Cassius Clay—I took him and his parents on a drive around Manhattan. It was snowing, and somewhere downtown on Second Avenue we stopped for gas. The station attendant was a huge black man; six-foot-six, maybe taller, real mean-looking. While he was putting gas in the tank, he was wiping snow off the windshield. Finally, I turned to Cassius and said, "Tell him that's good enough; close the gas tank, and we'll get going." So Clay leaned out the window and said, "Hey, man, that's good enough." And the guy answered, "Who's doing this; you or me?" At that point, all Cassius said back was, "You're the boss, man. You're the boss." And I couldn't let that pass, so as soon as he pulled his head back inside the car, I said, "Hey, wait a minute. All night long, you've been telling me you're the greatest fighter who ever lived; you're going to be heavy-weight champion of the world; you're not afraid of Sonny Liston. How can you let this guy talk to you like that?" And Cassius told me, "That man looks meaner than Sonny Liston."

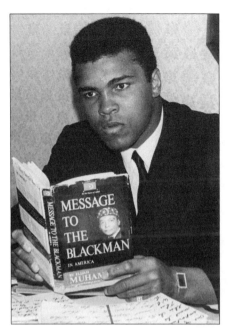

Betty Shabazz [wife of Malcolm X]: Cassius Clay asked my husband if he would bring our whole family down to Miami Beach [for the first Liston fight]. It was supposed to be our anniversary present. I was expecting, so my husband had to do some prodding to get me on a plane and to get our three little girls ready, but of course we went. And Cassius was a nervous wreck. He had a great deal of apprehension about fighting Sonny Liston. But my husband talked to him like a little brother and helped him conquer his fear. And this was after Malcolm had been cautioned not to go. He was told by Elijah Muhammad that, if he went, it would be on his own as an individual, not representing the Nation of Islam; and that, if he had good sense, he would stay away, because there was no way Cassius Clay could win. But Malcolm felt that, if Cassius Clay was totally focused on the fight, he could win. And one of the things he said to me was, "If he loses, he should not be alone."

Attallah Shabazz [daughter of Malcolm X]: I remember going down to Florida to celebrate Muhammad's birthday in January of 1964. The fight against Liston hadn't happened yet. But there was a birthday cake. If it had been a wedding cake, there would have been a bride and groom on top. But on this cake, there was the figure of Ali [then Cassius Clay] made out of sugar with both arms raised in victory standing over Sonny Liston.

Sol Silverman [the attorney appointed by the Governor of California to head a committee investigating professional

boxing]: The proposed Cassius Clay versus Sonny Liston heavy-weight title fight is a dangerous mismatch which could result in grave injury to the young challenger. Such mismatches not only endanger the overmatched boxer, but degrade boxing from a great sport to a sordid racket.

Cus D'Amato: I think that Clay has the equipment with which to beat Liston, provided it's used intelligently. Clay has speed and maneuverability. And if he employs an unpredictable strategy in applying that speed and maneuverability, I think he'll be able to confuse Liston and frustrate him and, after accomplishing this, be able to hit him with the kind of punches necessary to win the fight.

David Halberstam: I remember being very nervous the night Cassius Clay fought Sonny Liston. Clay seemed so young and vulnerable. And I remember caring about what would happen to him, being frightened that a dark shadow would fall over him, because Liston seemed to be what he was supposed to be.

Jack McKinney [sportswriter]: The problems Clay had with his vision in the first Liston fight were no accident. The two toughest opponents that Liston faced prior to Clay were Eddie Machen and Cleveland Williams. Machen lost a twelve-round decision to Liston and complained afterward that he'd been bothered by an astringent in his eyes, but he'd fought so poorly that no one believed him. Everyone thought it was just an alibi. And Cleveland Williams gave Liston all kinds of trouble in the first round. I was at that fight, and after the first round there seemed to be a lot confusion in Sonny's corner. In fact, he was late coming out for the second round because his mouthpiece wasn't in. He knocked Williams out in that round. And after the fight, Williams was obviously having trouble seeing. He kept rubbing his eyes. Later on, I kidded Sonny's cornerman, Joe Polino who was responsible for the mouthpiece, about the confusion. And Joe told me, "Someday I'll explain it to you." Well, I got my explanation at the first Clay-Liston fight. If you look at a film of what went on in Liston's corner between the third and fourth rounds of that fight, you'll see Polino in the ring with Willie Reddish

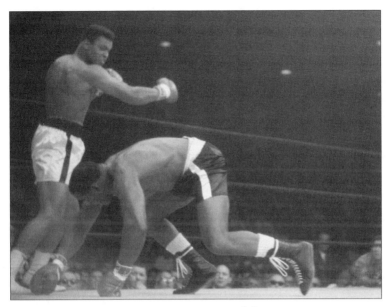

Sonny Liston tumbles.

[Liston's trainer] standing behind him, blocking everyone else's view. And Polino is at Sonny's knees, rubbing something on his gloves.

New York Herald Tribune **Editorial entitled "And Then There Was Cassius" [published on February 27, 1964, two days after Cassius Clay dethroned Sonny Liston]:** The clicking shutters; the stampeding crowd; the excited chomp, chomp as sportswriters ate their words by the thousands. It was a moment of glory straight from the story-books, as the one who had seemed an impossibly outmatched underdog stood victor over the champion; a moment that might have been wrapped in red, white and blue bunting and warmed the hearts of generations to come. But then there was the voice of Cassius: "I am the greatest! I am the king! I am the greatest"—shrilling to the world in tones that seemed to echo a thousand little Hitlers through all the ages of man, and the magic was gone. And instead of a champion, there was a boastful bully; instead of a sport, a spectacle. And it was sad. For one felt the loss, not only of what might have been a fighter's finest moment, but the loss of what might have been a hero.

Malcolm X: Brother Cassius will never do anything that will in any way tarnish or take away from his image as the heavyweight champion of the world. He is trying his best to live a clean life and project a clean image. But despite this, you will find that the press is constantly trying to paint him as something other than what he actually is. He doesn't smoke. He doesn't drink. He's never been involved in any trouble. His record is clean. If he was white, they'd be referring to him as the all-American boy.

Booker Johnson: Ali's father felt that he should be the administrator of his son's affairs. He and I used to argue. I'd tell him, "This is a different situation. You're dealing with lawyers and accountants, and your son has to have the intellectual equivalent on his side in order to deal successfully with them." After a while, he settled down and quit talking that he should be the administrator. But for a long time, he felt that he was cut off from his own flesh and blood. And it was a shame, because it should be a wonderful feeling for a man to know that his son is such a wonderful achiever and the most famous person in the world. What you should do under those circumstances is be proud of your son and enjoy his glory. But Mr. Clay blew a lot of that feeling. He missed out on a lot of the glory that he could have enjoyed, because he didn't understand that his son was an organization; his son was an institution. And the job of administrator was something that he just wasn't equipped to handle.

Robert Lipsyte [sportswriter]: In the 1950s and 1960s, people talked about sports as one of the few areas where black Americans could make progress. But the truth is, sports was a bastion of the old order. Black athletes could become stars, but they had to do it on the terms of an existing ruling class. They had to be grateful. They shouldn't go out with white women. They were expected to be dutiful and modest. These were men who oftentimes were egocentric, narcissistic, and very vain. But they knew the drill of dealing with the press. Never talk about yourself; always talk about the team. And now, along comes Muhammad Ali, who breaks all the rules and challenges that order. He's immodest. He's not sufficiently grateful to white America. He says what he thinks. And even though he's celebrated and people are fawning over him, he knows that, as far as white America is concerned, if he were still Cassius Marcellus Clay and not the heavyweight champion of the world, he'd be parking cars.

Angelo Dundee: I always let Cassius be Cassius and Muhammad be Muhammad.

Rocky Marciano: It's a very bad situation now, because there's a lack of respect for the present champion and that creates a lack of respect for all past champions. Nobody questions my fights; they were all tough ones. But people just don't treat you the same way since he came along.

Dick Gregory [political activist and human rights advocate]: A lot of people were afraid because he changed his name. You can't change your name. It's an awful thing to do to change your name. You don't believe that? Ask Coca-Cola. Tell them to change their name.

Muhammad Ali: God's got me here for something. I can feel it. I was born for everything that I'm doing now.

Angelo Dundee: Ali changed boxing. For a hundred years, the only thing fighters would say was, "I do the fighting; my manager does the talking." But then Muhammad came along, saying, "Hey, I do the talking. I'm the star. Nobody else talks for me."

Robert Lipsyte: Ali understood television. He understood the show, whether it was the poetry, the pre-fight weigh-in, or the fight itself. He was a born showman, brilliant at dramatizing himself. Whether he would have been the same phenomenon without television is hard to say. But he understood what television wanted; that instead of someone coming down, smiling, and shaking hands nicely for still photographers, television wanted the provocateur.

Angelo Dundee: Every day is like a new toy to Muhammad.

With Dustin Hoffman.

Muhammad Ali: I don't usually tell people this because they don't understand, but I don't have no fight plan. It would be the worst thing I could do to go in there with my mind all made up. I've been fighting since I was a child, and I do everything on instinct. Sometimes I wonder at myself when I see a big fist coming at my head, and my head moves without me thinking and the big fist goes by. I wonder how I did it.

Angelo Dundee: Ali did things wrong in the ring and made it look like art.

Muhammad Ali: The minute I'm hit, two steps backward, and I'm on the other side of the ring. Messages race out of my mind—retreat, retreat, danger, danger. I hear the messages and I'm moving away, but I'm still watching and thinking. It don't take long to clear your mind when your body is right. When you're in condition, it only takes ten seconds; then you're usually out of trouble. If he gets too close, just clinch him. Grab him, do anything. Stall for time, don't let him know you're stunned. Keep dancing with him like nothing's wrong; all this happening while the crowd is hollering.

Ferdie Pacheco [Ali's ring physician for most of his boxing career]: With the young Ali, boxing was truly "the sweet science."

Muhammad Ali: I'm so fast, I've got moves you can't even see.

Roy Jones: People talk about Ali's defense, but I think his offense was the key to his success. When Ali was young, you didn't have time to think against him. He was always putting pressure on you, because he could strike at any time. It was like, what his opponent did didn't seem to matter. And he had the safest jab I've ever seen because he didn't overcommit. He used his jab to keep you away and keep you in range until he hit you.

Muhammad Ali: I don't know anything about fighting, really. Only about me fighting.

Joe Paterno [football coach]: Ali would have made a great linebacker and an outstanding tight end. I don't know if he had the foot speed for any of the other skill positions, but his strength, quickness of hands, and balance were awfully good. Now maybe football wouldn't have been the right game for him. Certainly, at age eighteen or nineteen, he'd have needed guidance as to what he could and couldn't do as far as alienating his teammates was concerned. I'm liberal politically, but I'm conservative in terms of lifestyle and how I coach the team. And here at Penn State, we have a rule about players getting along with each other. You can only say you're sorry so many times. But I don't want to underestimate Ali's ability to accommodate any situation. If he'd made a commitment to it, I'm sure he would have been a team player. I know, I'd have loved the chance to coach him.

Muhammad Ali: Most black people in this country are mentally dead, and we don't wake up easy. It takes something like an earthquake to wake up our people. Oh, maybe black folks will get upset about something and burn a building or two, but in a couple of days, we forget.

Muhammad Ali: We were taught when we were little children that Mary had a little lamb, its fleece was white as snow. Then we heard about Snow White. White Owl cigars. White Swan soap. White Cloud tissue. White Rain hair rinse. White Tornado floor wax. White Plus toothpaste. All the good cowboys ride white horses and wear white hats. The President lives in the White House. Jesus was white. The Last Supper was white. The angels is white. Miss America is white. Even Tarzan, the King of the Jungle in Africa, is white.

Muhammad Ali: Things that are solid, black people don't think about that. They just dance and sing and go to church and shout. We never thought about doing nothing for ourselves. We depend on white people to grow our food and make our clothes. Used to be a sign on Miami Beach that said, "No dogs, Niggers, and Jews allowed." Jews got mad and united and bought the damn beach.

Muhammad Ali: I got tired of watching black entertainers on TV. Diana Ross married a white man. Lena Horne married a white man. Leslie Uggams married a white man. Lou Rawls married a white woman. And I said to myself, if God will just let me be big, I'll do it different. Because James Brown and Sidney Poitier and Diana Ross and Lena Horne and Eartha Kitt; them niggers don't talk to black people. They don't come through Alabama and talk to people. Niggers get big, and then they forget you.

Tom Hoover [a friend]: Ali's treatment of women when he was young isn't something that should be emulated. But the things he did right were more important than the things he did wrong. He made black women feel good about being black, the same way he made black men feel good about themselves. He made black women feel every bit as beautiful and desirable as white women.

Muhammad Ali: Whenever black athletes want to do something, white people run to Joe Louis, and Joe Louis always talks like the boss wants him to. Joe makes himself look real ignorant when he attacks me for standing up for my people. If Joe Louis don't like what I'm doing, he should discuss it with me behind closed doors. But instead, Joe Louis is making himself an Uncle Tom for white people.

Joe Louis: Clay has a million dollars worth of confidence and a dime's worth of courage. He can't punch; he can't hurt you; and I don't think he takes a good punch. I'd rate him with Johnny Paycheck, Abe Simon, and Buddy Baer. A lot of guys would have beaten him if he was around when I was. I would have whipped him.

Muhammad Ali: What's this about Joe Louis beating me? Slow-moving shuffling Joe Louis beat me? He may hit hard, but that don't mean nothing if you can't find nothing to hit. What's he gonna do when I'm jumping and sticking and moving? And don't say I can only do it for a minute, because I can keep it up for fifteen rounds, three minutes a round. Now how is Joe Louis gonna get to me? Would I just quit dancing that night and stand there and let him hit me? Joe Louis, you're really funny.

Oscar Brown, Jr. [who later wrote the music for *Buck White*, the Broadway show that Ali starred in during his exile from boxing]: My wife Jean and I and Jesse Jackson were over at Joe Louis' house. Jean, Jesse, and I were sitting with Mrs. Louis in the dining room. Joe was in the bedroom, laying in bed, looking at television. Then he came to the door, and said, "Cassius in on TV; Cassius is on TV." So we all got up to see Ali on TV. He was being interviewed, and he was saying, "I'm not an Uncle Tom like Joe Louis." He kept on ranting and calling Joe Louis an Uncle Tom, and I'm standing there with Joe Louis. I don't know how on earth it happened that I got into that position. The Lord just put me there, I guess. Joe didn't say anything. He just went on back to bed. But the next time I saw Ali, I made a point of telling him, "I can't stand to have the hero of my adulthood talking like that about the hero of my childhood. Joe Louis meant so much to us. No matter what you think, you have no right to say those things about him. You don't know what you're talking about. You don't know what conditions Joe Louis came up under. If it hadn't been for Joe Louis, you wouldn't be here."

Joe Louis Barrow, Jr.: My father was not very happy to hear Muhammad Ali call him an Uncle Tom. He didn't appreciate that. Joe Louis was very different from Muhammad Ali. He was a quiet individual. He was a humble individual. He didn't talk a lot. My father was not into mouth. He was not into being braggadocios. And he had a speech impediment, so he didn't articulate a lot. But he believed in this country, and he didn't like Muhammad Ali questioning what he felt. Joe Louis loved America. He knew that America had its problems. He was treated as an inferior citizen, and he fought against that in his way. He didn't picket; he didn't march. And he was criticized in the sixties for not being more vocal, but those who criticized him didn't have a sense of history. And frankly, I was disgusted with Muhammad Ali when he called my father an Uncle Tom, because Ali didn't relate at that point to who Joe Louis was and what Joe Louis meant to this country.

Jose Torres [former light-heavyweight champion and Ali biographer]: Ali and Joe Louis had harsh words for each other. They had different beliefs about religion. They had different beliefs about patriotism. But I think what really bugged Ali about Joe Louis was that Louis never gave Ali credit for being a great fighter. And Joe Louis was a great fighter himself, so he had to know how truly great Ali was.

Pat Patterson [the Chicago policeman who served as a security aide to Ali]: There were some hard feelings early on, but Ali and Joe Louis got to be friendly later. And there was one thing I've never figured out. When Ali saw Joe Louis, he'd start dancing and boxing, throwing punches real close to Joe's face, right in his face. "I'll eat you up; you're too slow; come on, Joe." Every time, he'd do that. Joe would move back, like he didn't want to be bothered, and Ali would keep it up; dancing around him, throwing punches real fast. It never failed. And all of a sudden, Joe Louis would reach out and slap Ali right upside the face. Bop ! A left hand, real quick. That would end it. And I never figured out whether Ali allowed it to happen that way or he couldn't stop it. Because, you see, Ali was a humanitarian, and he got a kick out of making you be who you were and making you better than you were supposed to be. So I don't know if he let Joe Louis slap him or not.

Muhammad Ali: I've been getting phone calls lately on my reclassification from 1-Y to 1-A. Reporters have been nagging at me. You know how they pick at you and twist things you say and make you say things you really don't know what you're talking about. They've been asking questions, and I have been with my big mouth, as usual, popping off. This time it got me in a little hot water.

Ferdie Pacheco: Ali's United States Army IQ score was 78. So what! Measuring Ali's intelligence with a standard IQ test is like trying to measure joy or love with a ruler.

Muhammad Ali: I'm against all war. I said that before all this draft-card burning stuff. I made a speech at a white college in Buffalo, New York. When I got to the room where I was gonna talk, they had thirty-four signs stuck up on the walls and behind the platform. The signs said things like, "LBJ, how many kids did you kill today?" So I told the man who invited me there, I wouldn't talk until they took all the signs down.

Reporter: Why won't you fight for your country?
Ali: I'm a minister of my religion, and this country has laws for ministers. George Hamilton, why don't he fight for his country? He's making a movie. Joe Namath, why don't he fight for his country. He's playing football.
Reporter: Joe Namath has a bad knee.
Ali: Yeah, ain't that silly. I saw Joe Namath playing football the other day. Twenty-seven passes out of forty-three is all he hit. Go talk to him about fighting for his country. I'm not using them as excuses, but you all keep jumping on me like I'm the last one; like you'll lose the war if I ain't in it.

New York Times **editorial [published on April 29, 1967]:** Citizens cannot pick and choose which wars they wish to fight any more than they can pick and choose which laws they wish to obey. However, if Cassius Clay and other draft-age objectors believe the war in Vietnam is unjust, they have the option of going to prison in behalf of their beliefs. Civil disobedience entails a penalty, but the risk is less than for those young men who willingly serve their country in Vietnam and other places of hardship and danger.

Reporter: Are you worried about not projecting a good image?
Muhammad Ali: What do you mean, project a good image? An image to who? Who don't like the image I project? That's the weakest thing I've heard yet; I'm not a good image. For my people, I'm the best image in the world.

Jerry Izenberg [sportswriter]: Ali against Zora Folley was the last time that the crowd at an Ali fight was comprised almost totally of boxing fans. Later, we saw the capes and gold chains and beautiful people and whatever. This was like the last hurrah for an era.

Howard Cosell: It seems to me that you're taking Zora Folley too lightly.
Muhammad Ali: Why would you say that?
Howard Cosell: Because every indication has been that you're confident you can beat Zora—
Muhammad Ali (interrupting): I'm confident I can whup all of them. This ain't nothing new. What are you trying to make it look like something new for? I'm always confident.
Howard Cosell: You're being extremely truculent.
Muhammad Ali: Whatever truculent means, if that's good, I'm that.

John Condon [director of publicity for Madison Square Garden]: When Muhammad was getting ready to fight Zora Folley at Madison Square Garden, there were a lot of public relations problems. But number one on the list was the fact that he'd indicated pretty clearly that, if he was drafted, he wasn't going to go into the Army. Then, about two weeks before the fight, I got a telephone call from Jack Hand of The Associated Press, who told me that Muhammad's appeal of his Selective Service classification had been unanimously rejected by the National Appeals Board. So I went over to Gallagher's Steakhouse, where Ali was having dinner. He and Angelo were leaving when I got there. I told them, "Let's sit down;

there's something I have to tell you." So we went back into Gallagher's, and I gave Ali the news. He didn't get excited; he didn't seem upset. All he did was look at Angelo and say, "Angelo, you better tell them to sweep out that jail cell, because it looks like that's where I'm going."

Barney Nagler [sportswriter]: Muhammad Ali has claimed exemption from the draft because he is mostly concerned with preaching the words of Elijah Muhammad. The Supreme Court must decide whether it accepts Elijah's teachings as a religion and Ali as a preacher of those teachings. The boxing commissioners, being students of comparative religion, long ago cast their votes against the only authentic heavyweight champion in the world. How easy it is to espouse the popular side of an argument; how much more difficult to stand firm in behalf of a cause believed righteous in the way Muhammad Ali stands. Ali is only a prizefighter, and perhaps too much store is put in the case of just one self-defined pacifist. But he has chosen to challenge a system that, he believes, deforms his people. And his choice is that of a man of principle.

Kwame Toure [formerly Stokely Carmichael]: Going to jail was my job. I'd been arrested twenty-five times in Mississippi and Alabama. So when they told me, "We'll send you to jail for five years," what I did was, I sat down and worked out a list of books that I'd finally get a chance to read. I wasn't worried. I'd get a chance to sleep; no telephones. I'm used to jail. I wasn't giving up anything. But Muhammad Ali had everything. Fame, glory, money, women, good looks, champion of the world. So when Muhammad would call me—we'd speak back and forth on the telephone—and he'd tell me, "I ain't going," I'd say, "Yeah, right on!" But I always wondered, when that final moment comes and he actually has to take that step, how will it come out? Because, no question, the FBI viewed Ali as more of a threat than H. Rap Brown and myself. Muhammad Ali had a broader base than we had. The government recognized that Muhammad Ali could cause more trouble than all of us. That's why we understood that the weight of the blow would be hardest against Muhammad Ali. They were going to take his championship crown;

no doubt about it. They were going to prosecute him; no doubt about it. They were going to do everything possible to bring him to his knees. And of all the people who opposed the war in Vietnam, I think that Muhammad Ali risked the most. Lots of people refused to go. Some went to jail. But no one risked as much from their decision not to go to war in Vietnam as Muhammad Ali. And his real greatness can be seen in the fact that, despite all that was done to him, he became even greater and more humane.

Muhammad Ali: When a man's guilty, you don't just say, "You're guilty." You hold court and prove it, and then you say he's guilty. You don't tell a man he murdered somebody without giving him a chance to explain and without letting the world see why you're condemning him. I never heard of them taking nobody else's title. People such as Sonny Liston have been in jail fifteen or twenty times. There's people with scandals, people who've been caught in their cars, breaking speed limits and carrying guns. And they don't get suspended, so what's the reason for suspending me?

Wally Matthews [sportswriter]: It's very difficult to explain to young people today how important Ali was, because the society has changed so much over the past thirty years. Now black pride is taken for granted. People understand that it's possible to be a patriotic American, and still believe that the war in Vietnam was wrong. And everything today is driven by money; particularly in sports, where athletes think they're making a sacrifice if they can't wear clothes with their favorite logo on them at an Olympic awards ceremony. I mean, how do you explain to a twelve-year-old that Muhammad Ali, based on an act of principle, risked going to jail and sacrificed the heavyweight championship of the world. Try explaining that to a young person today. He'll look at you like you're crazy; or maybe he'll think it was Ali who was crazy.

Ron Borges [sportswriter]: My father, who's eighty-eight years old now, isn't the most liberal person in the world. He was a construction worker for most of his life, and he never liked people who talked a lot. But when Ali was willing to go to jail for his beliefs, that got my father's attention. He told me, "You know, I don't agree with what this guy is doing, but he's all right. You get very few chances to be a man in life, and this guy takes advantage of them." And I'll tell you something else. My father voted for George Wallace in 1968 and for George McGovern in 1972. That's quite a change, and I have to believe that watching Muhammad Ali was part of what influenced him.

Reggie Jackson [Hall of Fame baseball player]: I remember how I felt when Martin Luther King was assassinated. There was no one to cling to except Ali. I don't know what I would have done if I'd had that kind of leadership burden thrust upon me. I do know that, ten years later when Ali lost to Leon Spinks, I was at my peak as a sports hero. I was Mr. October. And I knew even then there was no way I could begin to carry that load.

Muhammad Ali: I'm an easy target. I'm everywhere; everybody knows me. I walk the streets daily, and nobody's guarding me. I have no guns, no police. So if someone's gonna get me, tell them to come on and get it over with—if they can get past God, because God is controlling the bullet.

Jim Brown [former football great and founder of the Black Economic Union]: Ali is the only person I've ever seen who I knew was protected. Against all odds, he always came up with something because he's a spiritual person, and I don't necessarily mean religion. One thing I know for sure; you can't use logic when you talk about Muhammad Ali.

Oscar Brown, Jr.: I heard the term "exile" used in connection with Ali's inability to defend his title for a considerable amount of time, but I never thought of it as an exile. It was more just a ripoff and a robbery. Ali didn't go anyplace; he was still here. The title didn't go anyplace. The symbol of who is truly the champion of boxing is a belt that's got diamonds and stuff, and all through the whole period you're talking about, Ali had that belt in his living room. No, boxing was in exile. Boxing went away from its own standards. Boxing went away from its own creed. Boxing went away from the championship belt. It's nonsense to talk about Ali being in exile. Ali was right here.

Ramsey Clark [former Attorney General of the United States]: His independence was of a different order of independence; almost inherent, as if he was born that way. I'll bet you anything that, when he was five years old, he was like that. He just did what he thought he ought to do. He wasn't born to be forced; he's a totally independent human being. And to some people, that's very dangerous.

Bill Bradley [former basketball star and United States Senator]: Muhammad Ali was important because he was self-possessed in the best sort of way. The fact that he was heavyweight champion added to people's awareness of him and what he believed, but what was most admirable, regardless of his title, was his willingness to take a stand. That's something everyone has to learn if we're to become whole human beings. And because Ali did it, he was a powerful influence on many lives. Because of him, people became convinced that, if they stood up for their beliefs, they could prevail.

Muhammad Ali: Everyone has a right to their own opinion.

Pat Patterson: There was something about Muhammad that, once you were in his presence, it didn't matter what you thought about him; you reveled at being there. People who thought they hated his guts would see him, come over, and shake his hand. Even racist redneck bigots would hold out their babies for him to kiss.

Muhammad Ali: Life is strange. When I wasn't allowed to fight, it was the Jewish newspaper people [Jerry Izenberg, Robert Lipsyte, Stan Isaacs, Leonard Schecter] and the Jewish TV people [Howard Cosell] who supported me most.

James Earl Jones: Ali visited the set at Twentieth Century Fox when we were filming *The Great White Hope*. We got in the ring together. We were both wearing boxing gloves. The photographers were busy flashing. And Muhammad said, "Go ahead, hit me as hard as you can." Well, I'd played the Jack Johnson character since the play opened on Broadway. I'd been put through my paces by real boxing trainers. So I gave Muhammad my best left hook; he blocked the blow. And in the process, quite accidentally, he broke my thumb. You know, when a fighter like Ali blocks a punch, the block is devastating in its own power. I felt the pain immediately.

Muhammad Ali [after seeing _The Great White Hope_ on Broadway]: One thing is bothering me. What are they gonna do fifty years from now when they write a play about me. I wish I knew how it was gonna turn out.

Muhammad Ali [on his thespian career during his exile from boxing]: I was in a play called _Buck White_. The play was a flop; it lasted six days. But I was a hit.

A. Bartlett Giamatti [former president of Yale University and commissioner of Major League Baseball]: It is Ali who brought to the surface the actor in every athlete more successfully and obsessively than anyone else.

Gene Dibble [a friend]: Over time, I began taking Ali with me when my family and I went on camping trips. We used to go to the Indiana dunes, to Michigan State Park, anywhere, in our mobile home. Muhammad would help set up the tent, help make a fire; although to be honest with you, he wasn't much help. He didn't really know what he was doing out in the woods, but he was a happy camper.

Dick Schaap: In 1969, the year the Mets won their first World Series, I spent the last few days of the regular season with the team in Chicago. Ali was living there at the time; I was writing a book with Tom Seaver; and the three of us went out to dinner together. We met at a restaurant called The Red Carpet. I made the introductions. And of course, this was the year that Tom Seaver was Mr. Baseball, maybe even Mr. America. Ali and Tom got along fine. They really hit it off together. And after about half an hour, Ali in all seriousness turned to Seaver and said, "You know, you're a nice fellow. Which paper do you write for?"

Coed: Would you say you're the greatest?
Muhammad Ali: I don't say that no more. Would you say I'm pretty? Let me hear you.
Coed: I'm pretty.
Muhammad Ali: But you're not just asking me to say I'm great. You're asking me to say I'm the greatest. You say, I'm the prettiest.
Coed: I'm the prettiest.
Muhammad Ali: You're lying! [The audience dissolves into laughter] No, darling; I was just playing. Don't pay no attention. You're as pretty as you believe and as pretty as you think you are.

Howard Bingham [Ali's personal photographer and friend]: Ali had one of those faces that you could not get enough of. All you had to do was aim, and every photo was an excellent photo. You could not miss with Ali.

Kareem Abdul-Jabbar: Ali would kid me all the time. He'd say I was almost as good-looking as he was. That's the best compliment I ever got; someone saying I was almost as good-looking as Ali.

Muhammad Ali: Talking is a whole lot easier than fighting.

Hosea Williams [civil rights activist]: When Ali gave up the championship, he became America's number one role model in the black community. And when he came back, he truly convinced us all that, if you stand up and speak out for what is right, you will win in the end; that as tough as it is, even though you're black and poor, you can make it if you really try.

Bryant Gumbel: Joe Frazier was an available symbol behind whom people who hated Ali could unite. Was it Joe's fault? Of course not. In fact, one of the sad stories to be written about that era is that

Joe Frazier never got his due as a man. In some ways, he symbolized what the black man's struggle was about far more than Ali did. But it was Joe's misfortune to be cast as the opponent of a man who was the champion of all good things.

Joe Condon: Joe never liked Ali. He doesn't like him, didn't like him, and never will like him. But except for that one incident before their second fight when he went at Muhammad in a TV studio, Joe kept his feelings inside. He bottled them up, stored his hatred, and let everything out in the ring.

Butch Louis [boxing promoter and former "road buddy" of Joe Frazier]: Ali and Joe were like peanut butter and jelly. They needed each other to make things happen.

John Condon: You've seen the press-guide photo for the first Ali-Frazier fight; the one with Ali and Joe standing nose-to-nose, forehead-to-forehead. That was taken at Joe's gym in Philadelphia. I wanted something different, so I told both guys, "Put your foreheads together." And they did. Then I said, "Get closer; touch noses." But they wouldn't do it. So I went over, put their heads closer together with one hand behind Ali's head and the other behind Joe's, jumped out of the way, and told the photographer, "Get it!" And he got it. It was a great photo. But the problem was, it was so great that no one believed it was for real. Everyone thought it was superimposed. I had to show people the negative to prove it was real.

Dave Anderson [sportswriter, on Ali-Frazier I]: I've never forgotten the noise that I heard; the thunderclap of Ali crashing on the canvas about three feet in front of me. But as powerful as Frazier's punch had been, as flattened as Ali was, he was up at referee Arthur Mercante's count of three; up as fast as any human could be.

Bert Watson [business manager for Joe Frazier in the 1980s and '90s]: The first trip that Joe and I took together, we were driving in Florida and stopped for gas. We'd been talking about Ali. And right before I got out of the car to go to the bathroom, I said,

"One thing you've got to admit; the man was a great fighter."
Anyway, I go to the bathroom, come back, and Joe is gone. I had
to hitchhike to the motel where we were staying. Finally, I got there.
Joe was in his room. I went in and said, "What happened? Why'd
you leave me like that." And Joe told me, "When you work for me,
you don't say nothing good about Ali."

LeRoy Neiman: One interesting thing about Ali's appearance
is that he spanned an era when people wore big bushy Afros and lots
of facial hair, but he never gave in to that trend except for a few
weeks when he had a mustache. I personally took it upon myself
to tell him to get rid of it. Maybe, given my own mustache, I
shouldn't criticize someone else's, but he looked ridiculous. When a
prominent person has a certain look, he doesn't change it. Dwight
Eisenhower didn't start wearing a hairpiece. George Bush isn't going
to grow a beard. Except for the Army, Elvis Presley never got a
crewcut. In fact, most people, whether they're famous or not, tend
to keep their look. Maybe they make a few changes in deference
to the style of the times, but Ali didn't even do that. And he was so
extraordinarily good-looking that I thought the mustache was a real
detriment.

Pat Patterson: Ali could walk up to a piano and entertain you,
like you'd swear he could play the piano. He memorized how to
play a few songs, and he'd sit there and play just enough to impress
you. Little Richard was his favorite—"Bop-bop-a-lu-bop-a-wop-
bam-boom!" He'd play, and he'd sing; and by the time he got
through, you'd say, "Wow, this guy is really talented." But once he
did that, he couldn't play nothing else; not at gunpoint if his life
depended on it.

Cathal O'Shannon [Irish television host]: With Ali, there
was no way you could go wrong from an interviewer's point of view.
He was such a bloody showman.

Jerry Izenberg: I've never gone through the formality of playing
Russian roulette. But about as close as I ever came to it was getting

on a bus with Ali. You don't want to be on a bus with Ali for more than an hour. Because after an hour, Ali wants to drive and then you're in trouble. He loves to drive and he loves to drive fast. One time, we were in London. We were standing on line with everybody else to get on a bus. By everybody else, I mean the unsuspecting people of London, who were waiting to go home at the end of the day. Ali put his money in like everybody else and asked the bus driver, "Can I drive?" And the bus driver, of course, said, "Muhammad Ali, why certainly, you can drive." And the people on the bus were yelling, "Great! Great! Great! Muhammad Ali is going to drive us." And Angelo Dundee was saying, "No! No! No! Don't let him drive. You don't understand." But the will of the people could not be ignored, so Ali got behind the wheel. There was a terrific grinding of gears. The bus took off at a terrific rate of speed. And Ali had it pretty much under control, except for the fact that this was London, so while he was driving on the righthand side of the road, the traffic was coming straight at him.

Hugh McIlvanney [sportswriter, in response to Angelo Dundee's claim prior to the "Rumble in the Jungle" that Muhammad Ali knew how to beat George Foreman]: I, too, know a way to beat George Foreman. But it involves shelling him for three days and then sending in the infantry.

Harold Conrad: You know, it used to be the Belgian Congo. And then they had a revolution, kicked the Belgians out, and renamed everything. The name of the country was changed to Zaire. The Congo River became the Zaire River. Congo became a dirty name. But it was still a police state, and Mobuto had censors who read everything that went out on the wire. Anyway, the night before the fight, they had a big jazz concert in the same stadium where the fight was going to be. One of the writers reviewed it, and wrote about how great this guy was on the conga drums. And a censor changed it to the Zaire drums. I'll never forget that; the Zaire drums.

Muhammad Ali [to Stokely Carmichael (considered by many to be the originator of the slogan, "Burn, baby, burn")

as Carmichael entered Ali's compound in Zaire]: Stokely Carmichael, don't you burn nothing over here, or Mobuto's people will put you in a pot and cook you.

Ferdie Pacheco: Norman Mailer decided one night in Zaire that he was going to do roadwork with Ali. Ali told him, "If you want to run with me, you can. But I run five miles in the jungle; and if you get tired, there are no cabs to take you back. If you get tired, you'll have to run down the trail by yourself. I'm not going to stop for you, and I'm not going to send anybody back with you." Well, Norman was pretty potted by then, and he's afflicted by the need to always be part of the scene and assert his macho image. So about four o'clock in the morning, he went out to run with Ali. He ran for maybe a quarter of a mile, and then he fell behind, totally out of gas. In a jet black jungle. There wasn't even a firefly. Just total darkness. And then Norman heard this colossal roar. And if there's one distinctive sound in this world, it's the sound of a lion roaring in the jungle. That sound is distinct. You cannot mistake it for anything else. It's big and it's hungry and it rattles your bones. So Norman thought that his end had come. He didn't know whether to try to outrun it—he certainly couldn't outrun a lion—or ease on down the road, or just stand still and hope the lion went by. So he stood still for a while; and then he decided that, since he hadn't been eaten yet, he might as well try to get back to the compound, which he did. Ali had come back by this time. The sun was rising. And Norman told him that the literary world had come close to losing one of its great geniuses, because he'd almost been eaten by a lion. He's telling Ali, "There's a lion out there; you shouldn't be running." And Ali says, "Yeah, I know. There's a whole family of lions out there. They won't bother you." So Norman asks if Ali is crazy. And Ali takes him by the arm, and walks him down the road about a quarter of a mile to where the lions were caged in President Mobuto's zoo.

Muhammad Ali [acknowledging a dashiki-clad visitor in Zaire]: Welcome, brother. Do you speak English?
    Visitor: Yeah, I'm Tom Johnson from *The New York Times.*

Gil Clancy [boxing commentator and trainer]: George Foreman might have appeared strong to the rest of the world, but he had almost no confidence in himself. That was his nature. He wouldn't play you at anything, not even throwing coins against the wall, unless there was a stacked deck on his side. And that fight against Ali destroyed what little confidence George had. Without that fight, George would have annihilated Jimmy Young. He'd have walked right through him; but instead, Young beat him on points. Psychologically, that fight with Ali took away everything George had.

Jim Brown: After the fight, I went to Ali's dressing room to congratulate him, and then I went to Foreman's. Archie Moore was the only other person there. There was Foreman, Archie, me, and Foreman's dog. George kept looking in the mirror at the lumps on his face, as though he couldn't believe what he saw. Then we went back to the hotel, and George got a telephone call from Jim Marshall, who had been in three or four Super Bowls with the Vikings and never won one. Marshall did his best to console him. Foreman said, "Don't worry, I'll be all right." But you could see, he was totally bewildered by it all.

Jerry Izenberg: If you wanted to make an allegory about good and evil and patience and virtue, after that fight in Zaire you really could. It was like God waited until it was over. And then there was a tremendous clap of thunder, and we were caught in the worst kind of African cloudburst. It was the most intense rainstorm I've ever seen. If it had happened two hours earlier, the fight would have been wiped out. There were terrible winds, flash-flooding. And then, as suddenly as it had come, the storm was over. Dawn arrived; the sun came up. And it was like the whole history of "I ain't got no quarrel with them Vietcong" and the hatred and the ugliness had been washed away. And I remember that morning, standing with Ali by the Zaire River. There were just a couple of us. The air was sticky sweet with that aroma of African flowers, and the ground was damp from that tremendous storm. Ali was looking out over the river, and he said to us, "You'll never know how long I waited for this. You'll never know what this means to me."

John Condon: The "rope-a-dope" didn't get its name until 1975. Ali, [publicist] Patti Dreifus, and I were in an ice-cream shop at the Tropicana Hotel in Las Vegas right before Ali fought Ron Lyle. So we're talking about a point in time six months after he won the title from George Foreman. I kept telling Ali, "You know, this stuff you're doing on the ropes; you've got to give it a name. You've done it against Foreman; you've done it against Wepner; you're gonna keep doing it. Give it a name. So we're sitting there, and we come up with "on the ropes . . . if someone tries to hit you when you're on the ropes, he's a dope." And then we came up with "rope-a-dope." Ali's eyes lit up, and he said, "That's good."

Don King: Rope-a-dope is easy in theory. But in practice, it's a difficult thing.

Irving Rudd [boxing publicist]: You can talk about George Washington; you can talk about the Kennedys. But as far as I'm concerned, the closest thing to a king that this country has ever had is Muhammad Ali. And it's worldwide; not just here. If Ali went into a hut in Africa, a village in Asia, the outback in Australia, or a market-place in South America, the people would look at him, smile, and say, "Muhammad Ali."

Muhammad Ali: I have no power. I've got a cold right now that I can't get rid of. The biggest man in the world, struck down by a germ. I'm nothing, same as everyone else.

Muhammad Ali: Oxford University, that's a big university, wants me to be a professor of poetry and some kind of social something. They say I won't have to go there but once or twice a year for a lecture. And the salary they pay won't pay my telephone bills, but I said I'd come over for the prestige. Very few boxers can be professors at Oxford University.

Butch Lewis: Ali could convince you that his ice cube was colder. I mean, if he had an ice cube and you had one, his ice cube was colder than your ice cube.

Muhammad Ali: It's not the same anymore. Used to be, all I thought about was fight, fight, fight. Be the greatest. Be the champion. Now it's like I go to work, put in eight hours a day, do my job. I got other things on my mind.

Muhammad Ali: My intention is never to hurt an opponent. I didn't actually carry fights in a way that's crooked. But I will admit that I've seen opponents in physical unconsciousness on their feet and saw chances to really hurt them to the extent where it was possible to have a brain concussion, and I knew I was winning and the fight was just about over, so I backed off. I lost all my fighting instinct and hoped the referee would stop it. I don't like really hurting someone for the pleasure of a bloodthirsty audience. I'm a classy boxer. I don't want to kill nobody. I'm out there to box. All I want to do is make points.

Fred Graham [Host of the CBS interview show _Face The Nation_]: You have a reputation as a man who has a sharp eye for the ladies. What about this image as a womanizer? How is that going to be consistent with your role as a religious leader in the years ahead?
Muhammad Ali: As far as my personal problems with family are concerned, these are things I don't discuss in public; especially on high class shows like I was told yours would be.

Lana Shabazz [Ali's cook in training camp]: When Ali's children were growing up, he never wanted them in the newspapers or on TV. Partly, that's because he was afraid that, if someone crazy knew who they were, they might be kidnapped. But more so, it was because he didn't want any of them going around with a swelled head, saying, "Look at me; I'm important." That's what happens to children when they're in the papers or on TV. And Ali wanted very much for his children just to be normal kids.

Maryum Ali [the oldest of Ali's children]: When I was a little girl, the training camp was packed every day with all sorts of people. Sparring partners, newspaper men, celebrities, television reporters. People would come by the busload from New York. And I wasn't allowed in the gym. I had to stay in the house with a babysitter, because my parents were afraid that, if I went outside, someone would snatch me. I hated that. I wanted to be where the action was, and I couldn't be.

Leon Gast [producer of the Academy-Award-winning film *When We Were Kings*]: One time, we went down to Deer Lake to record Ali. This was between Zaire and Manila. Belinda was there; Ali's four kids were there. Ali's son was maybe three years old, and Ali was shouting at him, "Your daddy is the baddest nigger." The kid was trying to emulate Ali, but for whatever reason, he couldn't say "nigger." He'd say, "My daddy is the baddest nigo." Ali would say, "No! Nigger! Nigger!" And the kid would say "nigo, nigo." It drove Ali crazy. No matter how hard he tried, he just couldn't get his son to say "nigger." Then, later on, he was playing with the twins. He had identical twin daughters, Rasheeda and Jamillah. One of them was on his lap. He was kissing her, saying, "Rasheeda, you know I love you. You're the sweetest girl in the world." Belinda came out and said, "Ali, which daughter do you have there?" Ali told her, "Well, this is, ah, um, Rasheeda." Belinda asked, "Are you sure?" And Ali answered, "I think so." He was right, but he wasn't sure. And to tell you the truth, those girls looked an awful lot alike. I couldn't tell them apart.

Jerry Izenberg: Ali's grasp of geopolitics is limited. One time, he was in London to cut the ribbon at the opening of a supermarket. And of course, everyone there loved him. There were hugs and kisses and cheers, the usual adulation. Muhammad was quite moved by it all and said to me, "These people in England are so nice. I'll bet, in their whole history, they never had a war."

Dick Schaap: I learned a lot from him. I learned about laughing and enjoying and having fun with your work. I learned that life doesn't have to be solemn to be serious. He never believed all the myths and legends. He understood that a lot of it was show, and he would wink and let you know. He taught me that you can do so much with a wink. The athletes, the politicians, the people who

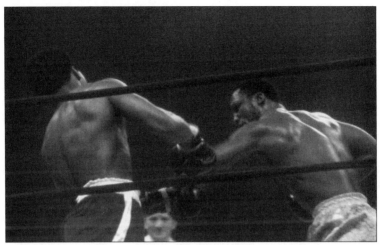

Ali vs Frazier I.

don't wink; they're the ones who should frighten you.

John Schulian [sportswriter]: Ali never gave anyone the same ride two days in a row.

Muhammad Ali: I was the Elvis Presley of boxing.

George Foreman: Muhammad Ali was the greatest showman in the history of sports.

Dave Wolf: It was fascinating how tight the security in Manila was [prior to Ali-Frazier III]. There was a curfew. And when Joe and Ali went out to do their roadwork in the early morning, it took place before the curfew was lifted. Somebody had a list of everybody who was authorized to run or follow in the cars. And if your name wasn't on that list, forget it. There were military people lining the roads where they ran. The troops could literally shoot anybody who turned up without proper authorization on the street. And it was typical of both camps that no one was curious about the politics of this. It was just taken for granted that there was some trouble going on, and whether or not the "troublemakers" were deserving of sympathy was irrelevant.

Butch Lewis: Joe was very self-conscious about his speech and his education. He came from the south; he grew up on a plantation. At one time, Joe was very hesitant to speak, because he took a lot of abuse about how he sounded and people maybe didn't understand him. And verbally, Ali would eat Joe alive. Joe was very upset about it. He longed to win some of those verbal sparring matches, but he knew he couldn't. The only way he could get even was in the ring.

Muhammad Ali: Joe Frazier is so ugly. His mother told me that, when Joe was a little boy, every time he cried the tears would stop, turn around, and go down the back of his head.

Joe Frazier: I don't want to knock him out. I want to hurt him. If I knock him down, I'll stand back, give him a chance to breathe. It's his heart I want.

Muhammad Ali: I got something new for Joe Frazier. I got a balloon punch and a needle punch. The balloon punch is a left jab, which swells him up, blows him up, puffs him up. And the needle's gonna bust him. That's the right hand. Whop!

Jerry Izenberg: Inside the ring, Muhammad Ali and Joe Frazier brought out the best in each other. And outside the ring, they brought out the worst.

Dave Wolf: It's possible that, by the time Ali and Joe reached Manila, neither one of them was the best heavyweight in the world anymore. Joe was nowhere near the fighter he'd once been, and neither was Ali. But as occasionally happens in boxing, their declining curves crossed at exactly the same spot. And they were so evenly matched and put so much of themselves into the fight that it was historic.

Muhammad Ali [in an Ali-Frazier III post-fight interview conducted while sitting on a stool in mid-ring]: I was surprised Joe had so much stamina. There was too much pressure. He's the greatest fighter of all times next to me. This is too painful.

It's too much work. I might have a heart attack or something. I want to get out while I'm on top. And one more thing. I want everybody to know that I'm the greatest fighter of all times, and the greatest city of all times is Louisville, Kentucky.

Bobby Goodman [a publicist for Ali-Frazier III]: After the Thrilla in Manila ended, Ali went to his dressing room and collapsed on a couch. He was completely exhausted. I told him the media was waiting for the post-fight press conference. And he said, "Tell 'em I'm too tired. I can't move." I'd never seen him like that before, where he couldn't do anything but lie there. But I had to do my thing as a publicist and get someone to the press conference, so I ran across to Joe Frazier's dressing room. Joe and Eddie Futch were there, very down, very depressed. I said, "Joe, I know it's tough, but we need you for a post-fight interview. Muhammad is finding it hard to get there. Can you help me out?" They said they'd do it. And that gave me the opportunity to run back to Muhammad's dressing room and say, "Champ, Joe Frazier's down at the press conference." Ali found that hard to believe. But finally, he said, "All right, get me my robe. If Joe Frazier's there, I'm gonna be there too."

Joe Frazier: Ali was the one who spoke about being nearly dead in Manila; not me.

Muhammad Ali: I got tired of seeing Joe Frazier in the ring. And I guess he got tired of seeing me too, because I whupped him two out of three times that we fought.

Larry Merchant: Ali was a warrior. He was in a hurting business, a hard business, the toughest game there is. And no matter what his style was, underneath it all he was one tough son-of-a-bitch. Most people never thought of him that way. If you looked at how people saw Muhammad Ali, that wouldn't be high on the list. But I'm telling you, in the ring he was as tough a son-of-a-bitch as anyone who ever lived.

Dick Gregory: We live in a society where we claim we don't want our children to drink. Even drinkers say they don't want their children to drink. But when the World Series, the basketball championships, any great athletic competition is over, there's always champagne. Little kids see their heroes pumping champagne, guzzling champagne, pouring champagne on each other's heads. And until Ali, you never heard praise to God. He was the first great athlete to show the world the importance of prayer. After his fights, right in the ring, the whole world got to see the spiritual Ali. When they put that television microphone in front of him, the first thing Ali always did was give thanks to God, and then the interview could begin.

LeRoy Neiman: I did a life-size painting of Ali once. It was eight feet tall. John Condon presented it to Ali at some big Madison Square Garden boxing dinner. When the dinner was over, Ali's not going to walk out with an eight-foot painting. So Don King said to him, "Don't worry, Ali. I'll take care of it for you and see that you get it." And of course, the next thing you know, the painting is in King's office at Rockefeller Center behind King's desk. Ali asked him about it at one point, but all he got was a lot of double-talk. And Ali acted like he didn't care, because that's the way he is. Then, about a year later, I went to Don's office, and the painting wasn't there. I asked what happened to it, and he told me Herbert [Muhammad] had it. Herbert had taken a shine to the painting and put the screws to Don to get it. And a little while after that, I got a phone call from Ali. Ali actually called me up and said, "Veronica [his wife at the time] really wants that painting." I told him Herbert had it, and he said, "Well, if Herbert has it, I can't get it from him. But if you call Herbert and tell him it's my painting, maybe you can get it." He gave me Herbert's home telephone number. So I called Herbert and said, "Ali really wants that painting. He must want it pretty bad, because he asked me to call you. And it's Ali's painting." Herbert didn't want to give it up. He said, "How do you know it's Ali's painting? I got it from Don King." I told him, "Herbert, I know it's Ali's painting because I gave it to him. I didn't give it to Don King. I gave it to Ali." Herbert said, "Well, Ali doesn't really want it. It's Veronica who wants it." And I told him, "Herbert, it doesn't matter. I gave that painting to Ali." Finally, after much pushing and prodding, Herbert sent the painting to Ali. Then, after the divorce, Veronica sold it to Joe Weider.

Jerry Izenberg: Jean-Pierre Coopman, who was known as "The Lion of Flanders," was probably the worst fighter that Ali ever fought. Someone involved in the promotion said to me, "Listen, don't be deceived. This kid can fight. He could hurt you." And I pointed out, "Coopman ain't fighting me. He's fighting Muhammad Ali."

Harold Conrad: Ali's old man was completely nuts. He always fancied himself a singer; always wanted to sing *The Star Spangled Banner* before Ali's fights. We never let him, but I got him a gig once. We were in Puerto Rico for the Coopman fight. They had a half-assed lounge in the hotel, and I asked the manager, "Do you want to have Muhammad Ali's father singing here?" The manager said all right. So we put him in the lounge, and he sang *My Way* every night.

Michael Katz: Ali looked awful against Jimmy Young, but I go crazy every time somebody tells me they think Young won that fight. You can't win a round by sticking your head out of the ring, which is what Young did all night. Each time a fighter sticks his head out of the ring, that should be a two-point round. It's like seeking shelter during the middle of a fight, and you're not allowed to do that in boxing.

Randy Neumann: I was a fringe contender in the mid-1970s. And the name of the game was, play your cards right and maybe you could make a couple of hundred thousand dollars by signing to fight Ali. Probably he would have beaten me, because basically I was a jabber and he had the best jab in the business. But if I'd gotten outpointed, so what. That happened in the gym all the time. And Ali wasn't an intimidating fighter like Foreman or Frazier who'd beat the crap out of you. In fact, at the end of his career, he was going fifteen rounds with guys like Alfredo Evangelista and Jimmy Young, and I was better than they were. In fact, I beat Jimmy Young, and Young almost beat Ali. So Ali was the brass ring that kept me and a lot of guys like me going. I'm sorry I didn't have the chance to fight him. I'd have made a fortune and had a ball.

Irving Rudd: Madison Square Garden wanted to match Ali with Duane Bobick in 1977. They even had a verbal commitment from Herbert to do the fight for $2,500,000. But then Bundini [Brown] got to Ali and said, "The Garden is trying to get you knocked off by a white guy. They want a white guy to win the title." So Ali told Teddy Brenner that he wanted Earnie Shavers instead. Teddy told him, "Shavers is a much tougher fight." But Ali was insistent, so they made Ali-Shavers. And while we were waiting for that fight to happen, Ken Norton destroyed [Duane] Bobick in 52 seconds. I watched Norton-Bobick with Ali and some of the other entourage members. And as soon as it ended, Ali got up, walked over to Bundini, and said, "You dumb nigger; you told me that white boy could fight." Slap. Slap. "You dumb nigger; what's wrong with you? I could have fought that white boy for $2,500,000."

Earnie Shavers: The Acorn. Yeah, I remember. You see, Ali nick-named a lot of the fighters he fought, and he called me The Acorn because of my shaved head. Well, Ali found out that night that The Acorn is a hard nut to crack.

Wilt Chamberlain: I always felt that the worst chink in Muhammad's armor was that he had no close friends who he trusted, who cared enough about him to give him good advice and help him in the right direction. If he'd had friends like that, they'd have told him, "The time has come for you to do something besides boxing. Use everything you've got going for you outside the ring, because right now whenever you fight you're getting your head beaten in." I know for myself, I've been fortunate to have friends with the balls to tell me when it's time to give something up or not do something else, and I've listened to what they had to say. And Ali had nobody like that advising him in the right direction. He fought long after he should have retired. And from what I've heard, he was used and continues to be used in ways that aren't very nice.

Al Bernstein: Boxing is like everything else. Nobody quits when they're on top. Frank Sinatra is still singing long past the time when he could sing. There are dozens of aging sportscasters running around, doing mediocre play-by-play. The only reason Steve Carlton and Tommy John aren't playing baseball anymore is that no team would let them. But unlike other sports, boxing has no cuts to make and it doesn't have to put its best players on the field. Promoters are happy to put anyone in the ring if they can make money off them, and most boxing commissions let them. So it's sad, really. Ali should have been one of the guys who got out okay, but he didn't. And in the end, even though it was his own fault, there's plenty of blame to go around.

Sylvester Stallone: The people around him were bad people. They used him as a payday and badgered him to go on and on long after he should have quit. They all saw him coming apart. It didn't happen in one night.

Bill Russell: I never saw him fight. I would never go to a fight. I just wouldn't. I went to one a long time ago and I told myself I'd never go back. They're much cleaner on television.

John Schulian: Laughter was constant when you were in Ali's presence. Yet as I think of the pieces I wrote during the last five years of his career, I cannot ignore the capacity he also had for turning a smile upside down.

Hugh McIlvanney: No one has been able to explain to Ali that fooling around with dreams of immortality can shorten your life.

Jerry Izenberg: Ali has a huge head. That made for wonderful photographs. But once his legs began to fail him, it also made a pretty good target.

Gil Rogin [former Editorial Director for Time, Inc.]: I was lucky. I never had a bad moment with Ali. I wasn't there at the end.

Larry Holmes listens to Ali.

Rex Lardner: It is one of the illusions of Muhammad Ali that, no matter how bloody the carnage in an endless series of battles fought, he will be the last to leave the field.

Hugh McIlvanney: The ring activities of Muhammad Ali now have all the grace and sporting appeal of Russian roulette played with a pump-action shotgun. The unquestionable lesson is that it is no longer his time. Muhammad Ali can still preach and philosophize, boast and charm. What he can't do is fight. The genie is gone from the bottle forever.

Jerry Izenberg: As far as Ali-Holmes is concerned, Ali had come to the right town. If you want to be deluded, go to Las Vegas. That's the place where, whatever you want, they'll pander to it. Whatever dream you have, they'll let you pursue it; but with the clear understanding that, when it's all over, the house wins. So if you wanted to dream that Ali could be heavyweight champion of the world again,that's okay, suckers. Pick a year and we'll freeze the calendar for you—until the bell rings.

John Schulian: What awaits us [in Ali-Holmes] may be a mismatch on the order of cockroach versus heel.

Alex Wallau: I'll never forget walking with Howard Cosell two or three days before the Holmes fight. There was an atmosphere in Las Vegas that gave Ali a chance. His physical skills had diminished, his reflexes were shot, his motor skills weren't the same. But there were intelligent ringwise boxing people who thought he might win. And I can take you to the exact spot in the parking lot at Caesar's Palace where Cosell said to me, "You know, Holmes is vulnerable to the right hand, and Ali has always been able to land the straight right. I think the old master is going to do it one more time." And I told him, "Howard, not only is Ali not going to win the fight, not only is he not going to win a round, he's not going to win ten seconds of any round."

Michael Katz: When Ali fought Larry Holmes, he wasn't in condition to shadow box for fifteen rounds.

Dr. Donald Romeo [who examined Ali for the Nevada State Athletic Commission before Ali-Holmes and okayed the fight]: So he takes some blows to the region of the kidneys and there's blood in his urine. Big deal. It clears up in a day or two; end of story. They talk of brain damage. That's a bunch of bunk.

Bob Arum: Greed is the essence of boxing. And it wasn't only the promoter's greed; it was the regulators' greed. The State of Nevada allowed that fight to happen.

Lloyd Price: I was in Vegas for Ali-Holmes, and it sickened me. I couldn't handle it. And what I thought about all through that fight was a day I'd spent in New York with Ali and Joe Louis maybe ten years earlier. Joe had been with me because there was a little bird singing in my band who he liked a lot, and Ali and I had been friends for years. Somehow or other, we got together and they were talking, mostly about boxing. I was listening. They got along well that day; no tension of any kind between them. And Ali asked, "Joe, tell me something. What happens in the ring when you get old?" He was asking about Joe's fight against Rocky Marciano, when Joe was 37 years old with that bald spot in the middle of his head, when he got knocked through the ropes and was counted out. Joe said, "Ali, let me tell you something. When I was young and wanted to throw a punch, I could throw it as fast as I wanted. But when I got old, my brain would tell me to do something and my arms just wouldn't do it." Ali was listening, but I don't think he understood what Joe was saying; not until he fought Larry Holmes.

Larry Holmes: Don't think that I went to bed those nights and had a good sleep, because I didn't. I was fighting Muhammad Ali. I knew I could beat this guy, but I never knew what trick he had up his sleeve. And it was mindboggling. Everywhere I went, there was Muhammad Ali. I got on the airplane, and who do I see on the airplane? Ali. I get to Las Vegas, and all these newspaper people, camera people, critics, who do they run to? Ali. We went through the casino, and all I heard was, "Ali! Ali!" And Ali could put a lot of things on your mind if you listened to him. He'd shadow box and show you how quick he was. He'd pull his shirt up and show you how thin he'd gotten. He was always saying, "Hey, I told you with Sonny Liston; I told you with George Foreman." And if you listened, you'd believe him. You'd say, "What the hell am I fighting this guy for?" So it was rough for me to sleep at night. I was fighting Muhammad Ali.

Sylvester Stallone: Ali against Larry Holmes. Oh God, that was painful; like seeing your child playing on the railroad tracks with a train coming, and you can't get him out of the way. I just sat there and watched. It was like an autopsy on a man who's still alive. And I also felt for Larry Holmes because he had a terrible job to do and he knew it. He had to go out and dismember a monument.

Ali, Leon Spinks and Don King.

Red Smith: If it had been any fighter except Muhammad Ali, he would have been thrown out of the ring and his purse withheld. Only a deity or a myth could get away with the performance Ali gave against Larry Holmes. Sluggish on feet of lowgrade clay, unable to throw a respectable punch or ward off Holmes' circumspect attack, Ali struggled through the unappetizing charade long enough to fulfill the contract worth six million dollars to him and then quit. When they speak of someone going out with a whimper, it's impossible to recall a champion or former champion who came up so empty at the end. There has always been a certain amount of con man in Ali along with his skills. Now only the con was left.

Lou DiBella [boxing promoter and former television executive]: Ali wasn't tarnished by his fight against Larry Holmes. By that point, Ali was above and beyond being tarnished by anything that happened in a boxing ring. But that fight tarnished boxing terribly, and it troubles me enormously that it was allowed to happen. Still, I have to say, it infuriates me whenever people use Ali as an example of why boxing should be banned. What would Cassius Clay have become without boxing?

Bill Cayton [manager and fight-film collector]: They didn't have "punch-stats" when Ali was fighting. But I've reviewed all the films of his fights, and they tell a story that's quite remarkable. When Muhammad was young, he was virtually untouchable. The two hardest punchers he faced in that period were Sonny Liston and Cleveland Williams. There was no clowning around in those fights. The last thing Ali wanted was to get hit. In the first Liston fight, if you throw out the round when Ali was temporarily blinded, Liston hit him with less than a dozen punches per round, most of them jabs. In the second Liston fight, Liston landed only two punches. When Ali fought Cleveland Williams, Williams hit him a grand total of three times the entire night. But if you look at the end of Ali's career, in Manila, Joe Frazier landed 440 times, and a high percentage of those punches were bombs. In the first Spinks fight, Spinks connected 482 times, mostly with power punches. Larry Holmes scored 320 times against Ali, and 125 of those punches landed in the ninth and tenth rounds when Ali was most vulnerable and Holmes was throwing everything he had. Those numbers alone tell you that Ali fought on long after he should have retired from boxing.

Jimmy Ellis [Ali's childhood friend and, later, WBA heavyweight champion]: We can all look back and say, "Well, Ali might have fought too long or he might have got hit too many times." But it's hard to give boxing up when you've been doing it for a long time, and you know you were good, and you know you can still whup some of the guys that's out there, but you just can't beat guys that's on a certain level. It was his decision, you know. He knew what boxing was all about and he knew what he wanted to do. He made his life what it was. And I got to give the man credit. He showed the world he could come back. He won the title three times.

Alex Wallau: I'd pick Ali over every other heavyweight in history, and that includes Joe Louis. Louis was a more complete fighter and certainly he had a better punch than Ali. But Ali had one

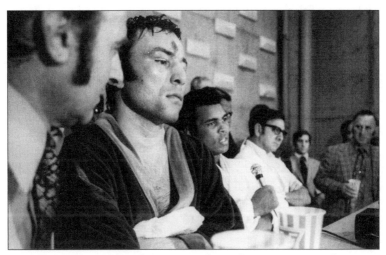

George Chuvalo awaits his chance to speak.

extraordinary skill that distorted the equation, and that was his speed. He had the speed to make opponents miss throughout a fight; and the few times they connected, he had the chin and heart to see him through. Also, Louis avoided a lot of tough fighters, particularly the other black heavyweights. And Ali really fought everybody.

Ferdie Pacheco: If you add it all up, Muhammad Ali reigned officially as heavyweight champion for less than seven years. There were three years in the mid-sixties before they took away his title; three years in the mid-seventies after he beat George Foreman; and a few months in 1978-79 after he regained the championship from Leon Spinks. But he dominated boxing for twenty years, and boxing isn't the same without him.

Ali's nicknames for opponents:
Sonny Liston - The Big Ugly Bear ("Because he's ugly and smells like a bear.")
Archie Moore - The Old Man ("He's old enough to be my grandfather.")
George Chuvalo - The Washerwoman ("He punches like a woman who's washing clothes.")

Floyd Patterson - The Rabbit ("In the ring, he's frightened like a rabbit.")
Ernie Terrell - The Octopus ("He grabs and holds a lot when he fights.")
Joe Frazier - The Gorilla ("He's ugly and looks like a gorilla.")
George Foreman - The Mummy ("George is slow. Clomp! Clomp! He moves like a mummy.")
Earnie Shavers - The Acorn ("He's got a shaved head that looks like an acorn.")
Leon Spinks - Dracula ("The man is missing his front teeth.")
Larry Holmes - The Peanut ("His head is shaped like a peanut.")

Muhammad Ali rates his opponents:
• The most skilled as a boxer—Floyd Patterson
• The scariest—Sonny Liston
• The most powerful—George Foreman
• The roughest and toughest—Joe Frazier

Muhammad Ali rates his fights:
• When I was at my best—against Cleveland Williams
• The best fight for fans—against Joe Frazier in Manila
• The fight that meant the most to me—beating George Foreman to win the championship of the world again

Muhammad Ali rates the greatest heavyweights of all time:
(1) Me
(2) Jack Johnson
(3) Joe Louis

Muhammad Ali's list of "The Ten Best-Looking Heavyweight Champions Ever": I'm number one. After me, it don't matter.

Dave Kindred: There's no cruelty left in him. As a fighter, it was necessary. As a fighter, you're supposed to be cruel. In the ring, if you're a nice guy, you get knocked out in a hurry. But that cruelty is no longer a part of him.

Jose Torres: The only bad thing that Ali left behind was his boxing style. His style—hands down, chin up in the air—is detrimental to fighters who try to imitate him, because they don't have the timing, the genius, and the magic that Ali had. So they try to imitate him and they get knocked out.

Earnie Shavers: Ali did things that nobody did before in life. Never did them after, neither.

Teddy Atlas: People talk about Ali being a hero. But a lot of people lose sight of the fact that one of the most heroic things about Ali was his almost complete unselfishness. I'll give you an example. In the 1988 Olympics, Greg Louganis cut his head on the diving board. And at the time, Louganis knew he was HIV-positive. Now Greg Louganis is a magnificent athlete. I give him all the credit in the world for his athletic skills and the fact that he continued to live a full life after learning that he was carrying the AIDS virus. But Louganis took the easy selfish way out. Instead of telling the doctor who treated him, "Look, you'd better get some gloves," he put his own personal interest ahead of the safety of the doctor. Now ninety-nine-point-nine-nine percent of the people in the world would have handled that situation the same way as Louganis. They wouldn't have jeopardized their public image or their chance to win an Olympic gold medal. But by acting the way he did, Greg Louganis knowingly put another man's life at risk. And I don't think Ali would have done that. Muhammad Ali always put other people first. And I believe that, if it had been Ali on that diving board, regardless of what it cost him, he would have told the doctor to put on a pair of gloves before he allowed the doctor to suture him up.

Harold Conrad: Ali is a decent man, a kind man, and it doesn't do you any harm to be around one of those. You've got to pick up some of it. Sometimes I wish I could be more like him.

Larry Holmes: If you treated Ali right, he'd treat you right. And if you didn't treat him right, he'd still treat you right. That's just one reason why people love Ali.

Dick Gregory: If people from outer space came to Earth and we had to give them one representative of our species to show them our physical prowess, our spirituality, our decency, our warmth, our kindness, our humor, and most of all, our capacity to love—it would be Ali.

Larry Holmes: Ali opens his arms right up to people. They don't have to approach him. He approaches them and makes them feel comfortable.

Earnie Shavers: Ali's got a heart as big as all outdoors and a love that encompasses all people. He's as pretty on the inside as he is on the outside. Always has been; always will be.

Dick Gregory: If I wanted to teach a little grandchild of mine about the universe, I'd go and get Muhammad Ali's story and say, "Here is what happened to the universe. One day, something went from nothing to BOOMMMM. The big bang. And it keeps getting bigger."

Lou DiBella: Ali's style has been taken to extremes in ways that I'm sure he never intended it to be. Now you have boastfulness and bragging, but with no sense of irony and no principles behind it. These guys—Deion Sanders, Barry Bonds, all of them—they just don't get it. Ali was the best "sound bite" in history. Ali was "prime time" before Deion Sanders was born. Ali did that schtick better than anyone; but with Ali, there was social relevance and substance behind it.

Muhammad Ali: When I was growing up in Louisville, I used to daydream all the time about being successful in boxing and being famous. But one time I remember in particular. Floyd Patterson was heavyweight champion of the world. I was at the Olympics in Rome and I went to sleep in my room, pretending I was heavyweight champion. This was even before I won the gold medal. But I lay in bed, pretending I was famous, pretending everyone liked me and looked up to me the way I looked up to Floyd Patterson. And God blessed me. My dream came true. But I got different dreams now. Now I dream about doing something to stop all the hating in the world. I dream about feeding people who are hungry. I dream about children learning how to read and write. And sometimes, when I'm really dreaming, I dream about being a rock star like Elvis or Little Richard.

John Thompson [former Georgetown University basketball coach]: In 1989, before the start of the NCAA tournament, I played a tape of Ali for the team. It was a tremendous piece, a documentary that I wanted them to see as an inspirational thing. Then, in the locker room right before the first game, I talked with them about motivation and confidence. And just before they went out on the floor, the kids put their hands together and shouted, "Float like a butterfly, sting like a bee. Rumble, young man, rumble. Ahhh!" Then the game started, and we came within a basket of losing to Princeton.

Kwame Toure: Muhammad Ali has a responsibility, and he knows what that responsibility is. His image must be used for positive reasons. His image must be used to advance humanity; his image must be used in the struggle against injustice; and his image must be used to harness souls toward a belief in God.

Jeffrey Sammons [professor of African-American studies]: One of the things that troubles me about Ali is his association with conservative Republicans. And finally, I came to the conclusion that Ali likes power; real power. In fact, I don't have any question about it. He likes the spotlight, the attention, the stage; that's part of it. But there has always been something more. I think Ali has always wanted power. When he was boxing, he had a legitimate power base outside of the political system because of his affinity for people and skill at media manipulation. Because of the political and racial climate, he was an important figure. But that political and racial climate has passed him by, and boxers rarely have much influence after they leave the game. Yet, in his mind, Ali still seeks power. And I believe he feels the only way he can have that power now is by associating with powerful people. But it's no longer on his own terms. It has to be on theirs.

Julian Bond: Watching Ali with Ronald Reagan and Orrin Hatch was worse than watching him against Larry Holmes.

Jerry Izenberg: During the [1991] Persian Gulf War, there was virtually no resistance from the Iraqi military. And as speculation about Saddam Hussein's strategy continued to mount, you began to hear that maybe he was conducting some form of "rope-a-dope" defense. Now the use of that phrase tended to obscure the fact that tens of thousands of people were dying. But it also said something about the way in which Muhammad Ali has transcended sports and entered the world's consciousness.

David Halberstam: One of the great things about this country is that you can invent yourself and reinvent yourself many times. And Ali was a true American original in every aspect of his life. I mean, really, what other country in the world could have created Muhammad Ali? If you look at his childhood, his rise, his complexity and contradictions, he's unmistakably American. He might be a Muslim, but he's a hell of an American too. And it speaks well for this country, not only that we created him, but also that we came to understand what he was about in time to admire him; that he's not a prophet without honor in his own land.

William Nack [sportswriter]: Even though he's still with us, I miss him. I miss his voice. I miss his sense of the absurd. Ali had a sense of the unpredictability and craziness and hypocrisy of life. I wish he was still running around, making speeches and doing all the other things he used to do. You know, in addition to being the quintessential civil disobedient and a walking lesson in decency and independence, Ali was one of the few people I know of who could make almost anyone laugh out loud.

Robert Lipsyte: Athletes die young. And ultimately, all athletes make a Faustian bargain that they have to pay off on in the end. So for the people who hated Ali, everything is fine now. He's a ruin, he's a wreck. And in retrospect, weren't they confident all the time that it would end this way as they moved on with their own civil-service kind of lives toward picket fences, retirement, and whatever else they think of as security.

Tim Witherspoon: One thing bothers me about me and Ali. [In 1986] I was getting ready to fight Tony Tubbs in Atlanta. And to sell tickets for the fight, Don King brought Ali in to spar with me. That's when people were starting to talk a lot about how Ali took too many punches and he's not coordinated and he's not talking right. Ali wanted to slow the talk down, so he sparred with me for a week. Every day, he had on a sweatsuit, headgear, mouthpiece. And in the ring, he's telling me to hit him in the head. "You can punch me; hit me hard. Come on, sucker, give me your best shot. Go to the head." In my mind, I didn't want to do it. But I was training for a world championship fight, so I went to his body pretty hard. I only went to his head a little bit. But I went to his body hard.

Ralph Boston: I'm not sure I'm good enough with words to express what I feel when I see Ali today. Maybe what I should say is, I remember all the chance meetings he and I had, passing each other in airports, heading in different directions. I'd see him through the crowd and wave, and he'd wave back, and maybe we'd talk for ten seconds. At the beginning, he was always so incredibly vocal and alive. But then, I began to see that he was getting a step slower and talking a little softer. And seeing him now—he's still alive; he's still sharp mentally—but it bothers me.

Dick Schaap: As the years have gone by, I think it's become harder and harder to be Muhammad Ali. It's probably the toughest role that anybody has had to play in the twentieth century. And to play that role twenty-four hours a day, day after day, year after year, I think that's taken as much of a toll on him as the punches.

Lou DiBella: I hear people talking about how they feel sorry for Ali, and isn't what happened to him terrible. But to be honest with you, I don't have that reaction. Sure, it makes me sad that his health isn't what it used to be. But he's still the same person. He still enjoys life. The sense of decency and principles that drove him in the 1960s still drive him. What does bother me, though, is the way some people react to Ali; like he's infirm or mentally deficient or in need of care. Watching people react to Ali like that depresses me. Seeing Ali himself is still very much uplifting to me.

Lonnie Ali: There are times when Muhammad allows his physical condition to take things away from him unnecessarily. He doesn't speak as often as he should, partly because he doesn't like the way he sounds, and partly because he can accomplish most of what he wants to accomplish by communicating non-verbally. Still, I have to say that Muhammad isn't as self-confident as he used to be, and still should be. Sometimes, I think back to how in love he was with the camera, and how in love the camera was with him. And it makes me sad to see the way Muhammad sometimes shies away from cameras today.

Betty Shabazz: Muhammad Ali has been a giver and not a taker. He lived life as he saw it. I look at his physical condition and I cannot bear it. I know he could have done differently; but he didn't, so we accept what he is. I hope that people will speak kindly of him, always.

Ralph Wiley [sportswriter]: People look at Ali's condition today and say, "That's sad." But they forget that, over the years, Ali punched a lot of people. He did damage to other peoples' brains too.

Joe Frazier: God has shut him down. He can't talk no more because he was saying the wrong things.

Muhammad Ali: I'd rather be punished here in this life than in the hereafter.

Julian Bond: Ali doesn't say as much now as he did before, but he doesn't have to. He said it all, and said it when almost no one else would.

Tim Witherspoon: When I see Ali today, the way he is now, I wish it wouldn't be.

Roy Jones [After a 1997 mock sparring session with Ali in which no blows were struck but a lot of strategizing went on]: When I'm fighting, the first thing I do is, I want to see my opponent's jab to find out if there are any flaws in it. The first time my opponent makes a mistake, I pick up on it. And the moment Ali and I started sparring, I could see he was searching for the hole, looking for a flaw in my jab. Right away, he picked up on something I do that I can get away with because of my speed. He thought it was a flaw and he found it. I've never seen anyone who could go out and search for the flaws that quickly. And I said to myself, this guy fights like I do. I run fights against guys like Sugar Ray Robinson and Marvin Hagler through my head from time to time. I have a strategy for beating all of them. So after sparring with Ali, I asked myself, "If I was fighting the young Muhammad Ali and we were both the same size, what would I do?" And I don't know the answer. If I was fighting the young Ali, I'd try to get inside his head, jab with him, go to the body. There'd be no sense in trying to knock him out. But then again, it would be very hard to outpoint him. In a lot of ways, it would be a tactical fight. But to be honest, against Ali when he was young, I don't see much that anyone could do with him. And I'll tell you something else. Sparring with Ali has made me feel better about where he's at today. Physically, he's still strong and a lot quicker than I thought he'd be. The man could get in a boxing ring tomorrow and beat the average person walking down the street easily.

Reggie Jackson: Muhammad likes me. I can feel him like me. I don't think he knows or understands or cares what I've accomplished in baseball. I've told him that I was called Mr. October, but that doesn't mean anything to him. He has no idea that I hit five hundred home runs or what that means. Still, I have to say, it's a nice feeling, to be liked by Muhammad Ali.

Ron Borges: I was in Miami for the Super Bowl a couple of years ago. It was a Friday night, and I was on a bus full of sports-writers who were about to leave for one of those big Super Bowl parties. Anyway, I looked up and there was Ali getting on the bus. The first thing Ali did when he got on was reach out and shake hands with the bus driver. And of course, not a single one of us on the bus except for Ali had in any way acknowledged the driver. Then we got to the party; we walked in and the first thing Ali did was shake hands with two waiters who were at the door. Don Shula saw Ali and came running over, but Ali stood there talking with the waiters, and Shula had to wait his turn. And that's the way Ali was the entire night. All the little people—the waiters, the busboys, the people that most of us never bother to think about—Ali stopped for every one of them.

Ferdie Pacheco: Ali has an awareness that he's somebody gigantic in this world. But the truth is, he's remarkably humble and it's not an artificial humility. As far as using ego in the sense of a Hollywood actor or some superstar athlete who's puffed up by his fame and self-importance, there's none of that. "I'm the great Ali; give me a hotel room." Never. "I'm Ali; get me on this airplane, even if you have to throw someone else off." Not a chance. He's just not like that.

Craig Hamilton [boxing collectibles expert]: I remember going to a sports memorabilia show at Hofstra University. Ali was there, and I had some photographs I wanted him to sign. He was sitting at a table. I handed him the photos. He looked at each one very carefully. And one came up; it was that famous photo you've seen of Cassius Clay sitting on a mountain of money. Anyway, Ali stared at the photo for a long time and then he asked how much money I wanted for it. And I said what I hope anyone would say under those circumstances: "Champ, it's yours." And I'll never forget; Ali stood up, put his arms around me, and hugged me like I'd just given him, not the photo, but the whole mountain of money. And that's the way Ali is. He appreciates every little thing that anyone does for him and doesn't think twice about giving away the world.

Lou DiBella: One night, several years ago, I took my wife to dinner in Manhattan. And as we were walking to the restaurant, I saw something close to a mob on the sidewalk. It was a crowd of people around Muhammad Ali, who was signing autographs. Anyway, my wife and I had dinner, and when we came out of the restaurant, Ali was still there, playing with kids, posing for pictures, signing for everyone who came up to him. I think about that now, when I look at today's athletes, who in the larger scheme of things mean absolutely nothing, who make millions of dollars, who won't take five seconds to give a kid an autograph. And I compare today's so-called "superstars" with Ali, a man in his fifties with Parkinson's syndrome, standing on the street that night, embracing every person he met.

Muhammad Ali: Every time I give an autograph, the person I give it to goes off happy and smiling and keeps my autograph forever. And to me, it's just a little thing, no more than a couple of seconds.

Dr. Dennis Cope [one of Ali's personal physicians]: In the end, what impresses me most about Muhammad is his extraordinarily charitable spirit. He's an incredibly giving man and always seems able to marshall the resources to help whoever might be around him. I remember one time when he was at the UCLA Medical Center. There was a patient in the hospital, an elderly man who was near death, who was a big fan of his. I asked Muhammad if he would go down to see him, and Muhammad said yes. We went down to this other patient's room, but he was off the floor for a procedure. I said to Muhammad, "Well, that's too bad; we weren't able to see him." And Muhammad said, "No, let's wait for him." We waited for half an hour, and the man still hadn't come back, so Muhammad said, "Let's go look for him." Finally, we found him. Muhammad talked with him for a while and then went back to the

room with him and they talked some more. This man's spirits were
so lifted by meeting Muhammad. I can't tell you how happy it made
him. He talked about it constantly until he died. I've been astounded
so many times like that by Muhammad's capacity to give. I've never
seen him disappoint anybody who wanted a moment of his time.

Lonnie Ali: It's gratifying for Muhammad to see the way people
respond to him. And what's even more gratifying is the way young
people who weren't even born when Muhammad was fighting are
drawn to him. These are five and six-year-old children who come
up to Muhammad and hug him. And it's truly a blessing from God
that the love Muhammad has for people and the love people have
for him keeps growing from generation to generation, and that every
new generation of children seems to know who Muhammad is.

Betty Shabazz: One of the things that has been constant
through Muhammad Ali's life is that he loves children. His children,
other people's children. I don't think that Muhammad Ali could have
too many children.

Maryum Ali: Everybody knows what my father was like when
he was young: the boxing, the controversies, I am the greatest. But
they don't understand what he's doing now and how deeply he
believes in Islam. As soon as he changed his name to Muhammad
Ali, he began making plans to propagate Islam when he retired.
No one took him seriously then. People said, "Well, he won't really
do anything like that." But he has. He meant it then and he's doing
it now.

Muhammad Ali: If I could go back in time, I'd like to be there
the day Muhammad received the first revelation from God and went
home to tell his wife about it. And I'd like to be there with Moses
the day he opened up the Red Sea; and with Jesus on the day of the
crucifixion to see if it was really him on the cross, because Muslims
believe it was someone else.

Roger Wilkins: I was the coordinator of Nelson Mandela's trip through the United States in 1990, and I was extraordinarily moved by the sustained love and joy that greeted him from one end of the country to the other. But after a while, it began to wear him down. Every big-shot politician and celebrity wanted a piece of him. They were all grabbing and grasping. Mandela went through it with incredible grace, but I will tell you, he was unimpressed by the behavior of many of the politicians and so-called superstars that he came in contact with. Then we got to Los Angeles, which is star-studded to begin with, and they turned out every star you can imagine. Mandela was more than tired by then; he was exhausted. We were walking together at yet another fundraising event. Mandela was leaning on me. And all of a sudden, I saw his face light up as I'd never seen it light up before. He looked past me, with a radiant smile. I felt his entire body straighten up and come to life, and almost reverentially he whispered, "Champ." And, of course, walking toward us was Muhammad Ali.

Alex Haley [author of *Roots* and Malcolm X's collaborator on *The Autobiography of Malcolm X*]: I see Muhammad Ali today very much as a spiritual leader. You know, here's a man who can go into the Islamic world, which is huge beyond our imagination, and you need troops to clear the way for him. I don't know if there's anybody on earth who could go to those countries and draw the crowds that Muhammad Ali can draw. To tell you the truth, and I don't mean to be irreverent, I doubt the Pope could draw crowds as large as Muhammad Ali. I think he's probably the single most powerful religious figure in this country, and maybe in the world, today.

Muhammad Ali: If you love God, you can't separate out and love only some of His children. To be against people because they're Muslim is wrong. To be against people because they're Christian or Jewish is wrong. To be against people because they're black or white or yellow or brown is wrong. Anyone who believes in One God should also believe that all people are part of one family. People are people. God created us all.

Ramsey Clark: To me, Muhammad Ali is a totally spiritual person. It doesn't have to do with the Christian faith in which he was raised, and it doesn't have to do with the Islamic faith to which he converted; both great religions. It has to do with his love for life, his faith in the human spirit, and his belief in the equality of all people. I see Ali as a human being whose sense of purpose in life is to help others. He must lay awake at night, wondering what he can do to help people, because wherever people are in need, his priorities are there. He sees children who are right next to him, but children who are starving in Africa and threatened by bombing in Iraq are also within the scope of his imagination. He wants to help everyone and he travels at great personal burden and financial expense to be wherever he's needed. And I say, God bless him. He makes an enormous difference.

Muhammad Ali: Life is short; we get old so fast. It doesn't make sense to waste time on hating.

Ferdie Pacheco: I'm sure that God looks down on Ali from time to time, shakes his head in wonderment, and smiles.

Bill Clinton: Muhammad Ali taught us all that, whatever color you are, whatever religion you are, you can be proud of who you are.

Jerry Izenberg: This is a man who spent his whole life telling the world, "I Am The Greatest!" And whenever you got exasperated with him and said, "Shut up, because you're not," he'd do something to prove that he was.

Ralph Boston: There are lots good athletes and a few great athletes. But there's only one Ali.

Dave Kindred: Rainbows are born of thunderstorms. Muhammad Ali is both.

Jerry Izenberg: People don't really think of Ali as being black anymore. He's one of a kind; he's Muhammad Ali. And that's the wonderful ultimate irony; that this man who was once viewed as a dangerous militant black-nationalist revolutionary should turn out to be without color in the eyes of America.

Ralph Boston: If a young boy were to ask me today, "Why should I care about Muhammad Ali?" I'd tell him, "Because Ali cares about you." That might be hard for some people to understand, but that's the way Ali is. He cares about every single person on this planet.

John Carlos: Muhammad Ali is love.

Ali and Kris Kristofferson in 1979's *Freedom Road.*

THE LOST LEGACY
OF MUHAMMAD ALI

The Lost Legacy of Muhammad Ali

(2005)

In 1960, shortly after the Rome Olympics, a Soviet journalist asked Cassius Marcellus Clay, Jr. how it felt to win a gold medal for his country when there were restaurants in the United States that he was forbidden to eat in. Clay's response was short and sweet: "Tell your readers we got qualified people working on that problem. To me, the USA is the best country in the world, including yours."

Seven years later, that same young man was one of the most vilified personages in America.

People today understand that Muhammad Ali defied the United States government and alienated mainstream America because he stood up for his principles. But they don't know what those principles were. Generally, they are aware that, after beating Sonny Liston to capture the heavyweight championship in 1964, Clay announced that he had accepted the teachings of a religion known as the Nation of Islam and changed his name to Muhammad Ali. Thereafter, he refused induction into the United States Army during the height of the war in Vietnam. But to younger generations, Ali today is famous primarily for being famous. There has been a deliberate distortion of what he once believed, said, and stood for. History is being rewritten to serve political, social, and economic ends.

Thus, it's important to revisit the Muhammad Ali who, in the words of author Dave Kindred, was "as near to living flame as a man can get."

In the early 1960s, when Ali first entered the public consciousness, sports was considered one of the few areas where black Americans could compete on equal footing with whites. But in reality, sports reflected the old order. Black athletes could become stars, but only within guidelines dictated by the establishment. And away from the playing fields, as Ali himself once noted, "Many colored people thought it was better to be white." Black Americans were scorned, demeaned, and denied even self-love.

In 1961, while in Florida training for a fight, Cassius Clay met a man named Sam Saxon. Saxon was one of a small group of adherents (known to the media as "Black Muslims") who attended Nation of Islam meetings at a Miami temple and followed the black separatist teachings of a self-proclaimed "messenger" named Elijah Muhammad. Clay accepted Saxon's invitation to attend a Nation of Islam service, and thereafter was indoctrinated with the tenets of the religion.

The Nation of Islam taught that white people were devils who had been genetically created by an evil scientist with a big head named Mr. Yacub. It maintained that there was a wheel-shaped Mother of Planes one-half mile wide manned by black men in the sky, and that, on Allah's chosen day of retribution, fifteen hundred planes from the Mother of Planes would drop deadly explosives destroying all but the righteous on earth. Neither of these views are part of traditional Islamic thought or find justification in the Qur'an. Moreover, while the concepts of Heaven and Hell are central to traditional Islamic doctrine, the National of Islam rejected both.

Herbert Muhammad, one of Elijah Muhammad's sons, later explained and sought to defend his father's teachings as follows:

> Black people knew their life was bad. They wanted something to make it better. And my father's message was to gain dignity and self respect and make black people the master of their own needs. As long as other people controlled what we needed, then these people would be able to control us. So my father sought to make black people self reliant and take them away from gambling, alcohol, prostitution, and drugs. He taught us that the answer to what black people need is in God and in

ourselves. And you have to ask what it was that enabled my father to get a man or woman off drugs when right now the whole government can't do it. You have to ask what it was that could bring a man out of prison, and the next month have that man be clean-shaven, wearing clean clothes, completely clean. You see, my father saw that black people had a deep inferiority complex. He saw that white people had a great superiority complex. And by the whites being in an upper-hand position, blacks would never come up unless someone gave them a philosophy that they were better than whites.

From 1964 through his conversion to orthodox Islam in 1975, Muhammad Ali was the Nation of Islam's most visible and vocal spokesman in America. Nation of Islam teachings were at the core of who he was at that time in his life. Among the positions Ali preached were:

On integration: "We who follow the teachings of Elijah Muhammad don't want to force integrate. Integration is wrong. We don't want to live with the white man; that's all."

On intermarriage: "No intelligent black man or black woman in his or her right black mind wants white boys and white girls coming to their homes to marry their black sons and daughters."

On the need for a separate black homeland: "Why don't we get out and build our own nation? White people just don't want their slaves to be free. That's the whole thing. Why not let us go and build ourselves a nation? We want a country. We're forty million people, but we'll never be free until we own our own land."

On brotherhood: "We're not all brothers. You can say we're brothers, but we're not."

Ali was black and proud of it at a time when many black Americans were running from their color. "He lived a lot of lives for a lot of people," said social activist Dick Gregory. "And he was able to tell white folks for us to go to hell."

For more than a decade, Ali was the gloved fist of John Carlos and Tommie Smith every day of the year. The establishment media, and sportswriters in particular, came down hard on him. Jim Murray of the *Los Angeles Times* labeled Ali the "white man's burden." Jimmy Cannon of the *New York Journal American* called his ties to the Nation of Islam "the dirtiest in American sports since the Nazis were shilling for Max Schmeling as representative of their vile theories of blood."

A lot of white liberals and black Americans also took issue with Ali. "I never went along with the pronouncements of Elijah Muhammad that the white man was the devil and that blacks should be striving for separate development; a sort of American apartheid," said Arthur Ashe. "That never made sense to me. It was a racist ideology, and I didn't like it."

Joe Louis added his voice to those opposing Ali and opined, "I'm against Black Muslims. I've always believed that every man is my brother. Clay will earn the public's hatred because of his connections with the Black Muslims. The things they preach are just the opposite of what we believe."

Former heavyweight champion Floyd Patterson concurred with Louis, declaring, "I've been told that Clay has every right to follow any religion he chooses, and I agree. But by the same token, I have every right to call the Black Muslims a menace to the United States and a menace to the Negro race. I do not believe God put us here to hate one another. I believe the preaching of segregation, hatred, rebellion, and violence is wrong. Cassius Clay is disgracing himself and the Negro race."

Still, whether or not one liked what Ali represented, it was clear that his demand for full entitlement for all black people was on the cutting edge of an era. And to many, he was the ultimate symbol of black pride and black resistance to an unjust social order. In that vein, Jeremiah Shabazz, who was one of Ali's first teachers within the Nation of Islam, recalled, "When Elijah Muhammad spoke, his words were confined to whatever city he had spoken in. But Ali was a sports hero and people wanted to hear what he had to say, so his visibility and prominence were of great benefit. His voice carried throughout the world."

Outside the ring, Ali was never violent. His threat to the status quo was one of ideas, which is ironic because he himself was never a "thinker." But beneath it all, there was fear within the establishment that the ideas Ali preached could be converted to rebellion in the streets. Indeed, one can make the case that Ali and the Nation of Islam frightened the powers that be in America into embracing the agenda of moderate civil rights leaders as a way of muting the cries of those who wanted more.

Arthur Ashe later recalled, "I can tell you that Ali was very definitely, sometimes unspokenly, admired by a lot of the leaders of the civil rights movement, who were sometimes even a little bit jealous of the following he had and the efficacy of what he did. There were a lot of people in the movement who wished that they held that sort of sway over African-Americans but did not."

"Muhammad was probably the first black man in America to successfully break with the white establishment and survive," posited civil rights pioneer Andrew Young.

And before Cassius Clay ever changed his name, Malcolm X maintained, "Clay will mean more to his people than Jackie Robinson, because Robinson is the white man's hero but Cassius is the black man's hero."

"It's very difficult to imagine being young and black in the sixties and not gravitating toward Ali," Bryant Gumbel later recalled. "He was a guy who was supremely talented, enormously confident, and seemed to think less of what the establishment thought of him than about the image he saw when he looked in the mirror. And to people who were young and black and interested in tweaking the establishment, and in some cases shoving it up the tail of the establishment, you had to identify with somebody like that. The fact that he won all the time made it even better. You know, for all our passions of those years, we didn't have a lot of victories. More often than not, we were on the losing side, so the fact that Ali won was gravy. He was a heroic figure plain and simple. In every sense of the word, he was heroic."

The civil rights movement and Ali as a fighter both peaked in the mid-1960s. Then the war in Vietnam intervened.

In 1964, Ali had been classified 1-Y (not qualified for military service) as a result of scoring poorly on a Selective Service mental aptitude examination. Then, in early 1966, with the war expanding and manpower needs growing, the test score required for induction into the armed forces was lowered, leaving him eligible for the draft. Ali requested a deferment, but on February 17, 1966, his request was denied and he was reclassified 1-A (available for the draft). Several hours later, a frustrated Ali blurted out to reporters, "I ain't got no quarrel with them Vietcong."

The following day, Ali's outburst was front-page news across the country, and the sporting press raged against him. Red Smith of *The New York Times* harangued, "Squealing over the possibility that the military may call him up, Cassius makes himself as sorry a spectacle as those unwashed punks who picket and demonstrate against the war." Jimmy Cannon continued the assault, proclaiming, "Clay is part of the Beatle movement. He fits in with the famous singers no one can hear and the punks riding motorcycles with iron crosses pinned to their leather jackets and the boys with their long dirty hair and the girls with the unwashed look and the college kids dancing naked at secret proms held in apartments and the revolt of students who get a check from dad every first of the month and the painters who copy the labels off soup cans and the surf bums who refuse to work and the whole pampered style-making cult of the bored young."

Ali wasn't a political thinker. His initial concern over being drafted wasn't religious or political. It was that of a twenty-four-year-old who thought he had put the draft behind him and then learned that he was in danger of having his life turned upside down.

"Muhammad never studied day-to-day current events like the thousands of white kids who opposed the war," Jeremiah Shabazz later acknowledged. "But even though he was unsophisticated in his thinking, he knew it was a senseless unjust war. And of course, in addition to that, Muslims following the Honorable Elijah Muhammad decided long ago that we weren't going to fight the white man's wars. If he starts them, he can fight them."

On April 28, 1967, citing his religious beliefs, Ali refused induction into the United States Army. "Clay seems to have gone past the borders of faith," Milton Gross wrote in the *New York Post.* "He has reached the boundaries of fanaticism."

Less than eight weeks later, on June 20th, Ali was convicted of refusing induction into the armed forces and sentenced to five years in prison. He was stripped of his title and precluded by state athletic commissions throughout the country from fighting. His "exile" from boxing lasted for more than three years.

Ali's refusal to accept induction was part and parcel of a schism within the civil rights movement. "The more conservative black leadership was troubled by his opposition to the war," Julian Bond later recalled. "The civil rights movement at that time was split. There was one group of people who said, 'Let's not have any opinion about the war because this will alienate us from the powers that be, from President Johnson and successor presidents.' And there was another group that said, 'Listen, this war is wrong. It's killing black people disproportionately; it's draining resources that could be applied to the war on poverty; it's wrong in every respect.' So people in the first group were horrified by Ali. They thought he was a dunce manipulated by the Nation of Islam. And those in the second group felt entirely differently about him. Still," Bond continued, "it's hard to imagine that a sports figure could have so much political influence on so many people. When a figure as heroic and beloved as Muhammad Ali stood up and said, 'No, I won't go,' it reverberated through the whole society. People who had never thought about the war before began to think it through because of Ali. The ripples were enormous."

Andrew Young had similar memories in recalling the reaction of his own mentor, Martin Luther King, Jr., to Ali's decision. "Martin made his most publicized speech against the war in Vietnam at Riverside Church [in New York] on April 4, 1967, exactly one year to the day before he was assassinated," Young remembered. "It was soon after that speech that Muhammad refused to take the step forward, and I know Martin was very proud of him."

However, others within the black community took a lesser view of Ali's conduct. "He's hurting the morale of a lot of young Negro soldiers over in Vietnam," said Jackie Robinson. "And the tragedy to me is, Cassius has made millions of dollars off of the American public, and now he's not willing to show his appreciation to a country that's giving him a fantastic opportunity." Joe Louis was in accord with his baseball counterpart, saying, "Anybody in America who don't want to fight for this country; I think it's very bad, especially a guy who has made a lot of money in this country. I was champion at the time World War II started; and when my time came up, I had to go. I think that he should fight for his country."

More significantly, though, Vietnam deflected attention from Ali's racial views and put him in a context where many whites and white opinion-makers could identify with him. There had been an ugly mood around Ali, starting with the assassination of Malcolm X in February 1965. Thereafter, Ali seemed to take on a bit of the persona, not just the ideology, of the Nation of Islam. But when the spotlight turned from Ali's acceptance of an ideology that sanctioned hate to his refusal to accept induction into the United States Army, he began to bond with the white liberal community which at the time was quite strong.

Thus it was that Ali was martyred and lived to talk about it. Ultimately, he returned to boxing. After wins against Jerry Quarry and Oscar Bonavena, he lost a historic fifteen-round decision to Joe Frazier at Madison Square Garden. Then his conviction for refusing induction into the United States Army was reversed by the United States Supreme Court on a procedural technicality. After that, Ali reeled off ten more victories but suffered a broken jaw in a twelve-round loss to Ken Norton. That made him an "underdog" in the eyes of America. People who had once bristled at his words and conduct began to feel sorry for him.

Ali earned a measure of revenge against Frazier and Norton with victories in hard-fought rematches. Then, on October 30, 1974, he dethroned George Foreman to recapture the heavyweight championship of the world. But more importantly, by that time, America had turned against the war in Vietnam. It was clear that Ali had sacrificed enormously for his beliefs. And whether or not people liked the racial component of Ali's views, there was respect for the fact that he had stood by them.

On December 10, 1974, Ali was invited to the White House by President Gerald Ford. It was an occasion that would have been unthinkable several years earlier and marked a turning point in the country's embrace of Ali.

Then, on February 25, 1975, Elijah Muhammad died.

"After Elijah died," Ali said later, "his son Wallace took over as leader. That didn't surprise us, because we'd been told Wallace would come after his father. But what surprised some people was, Wallace changed the direction of the Nation. He'd learned from his studies that his father wasn't teaching true Islam, and Wallace taught us the true meaning of the Qur'an."

Elijah Muhammad's death marked a seismic shift for the Nation of Islam and foreshadowed a significant change in Ali's public pronouncements on race. In the past, the public and private Ali had seemed almost at war with one another over whether white people were truly evil. Now Ali was able to say openly, "I don't hate whites. That was history, but it's coming to an end."

Some of Elijah Muhammad's adherents refused to accept the teachings of his son, Wallace. Ministers like Jeremiah Shabazz and Louis Farrakhan maintained that Elijah had been a prophet and continued to preach what he had taught them. Meanwhile, Ali's religious views were evolving and he later acknowledged, "When I was young, I followed a teaching that disrespected other people and said that white people were devils. I was wrong. Color doesn't make a man a devil. It's the heart and soul and mind that count. What's on the outside is only decoration. Hating someone because of his color is wrong. It's wrong both ways; it don't matter which color does the hating. All people, all colors, got to work to get along."

Ali is now a living embodiment of Martin Luther King, Jr.'s message that all people are deserving of love. As Jerry Izenberg, one of America's foremost sports journalists, observed, "Ironically, after all he went through, the affection for Ali is largely colorblind. Late in his career, he developed a quality that only a few people have. He reached a point where, when people looked at him, they didn't see black or white. They saw Ali. For a long time, that mystified him. He expected black people to love him and crowd around him, but then he realized white people loved him too; and that made him very happy."

Ali's love affair with America and the world reached its zenith in 1996. Fifteen years earlier, his public profile had dropped after his retirement from boxing. Thereafter, if Ali appeared at an event, those in attendance were excited but he wasn't on the national radar screen.

Then Ali was chosen to light the Olympic flame in Atlanta. It was a glorious moment. Three billion people around the world watched on television and were united by love and caring for one man. But there's a school of thought that the 1996 Olympics carried negatives as well, for it was in Atlanta that corporate America "rediscovered" Ali. And since then, there has been a determined effort to rewrite history. In order to take advantage of Ali's economic potential, it has been deemed desirable to "sanitize" him. And as a result, all of the "rough edges" are being filed away from Ali's life story.

"Commercialization is a natural process in this country," says Jerry Izenberg. "But the Ali I fell in love with wasn't for sale. He fought the good fight in and out of the ring, and that was payment enough for him. He wasn't looking to get paid in dollars, and the true worth of the stands he made wasn't commercial. Then corporate America latched onto Ali at the Olympics," Izenberg continues, "and he became a gravy train for everyone who wants to make a movie or sell something to the public. But the public gains nothing when Ali is commercialized and marketed the way he is today."

No event crystallized the commercialization of Ali more clearly than his appearance at the New York Stock Exchange on December 31, 1999. That was an important day. By most reckonings, it marked the end of a millennium. The Ali who won hearts in the 1960s could have been expected to celebrate the occasion at a soup kitchen or homeless shelter to draw attention to the plight of the disadvantaged. Many hoped to see Ali spend December 31, 1999, in a spiritual setting. Instead, the man who decades earlier was a beacon of hope for oppressed people around the globe and who refused to become a symbol for the United States Army became a symbol for the New York Stock Exchange.

"If it [the stock market] goes up, then you will have been blessed by my presence," Ali told the assembled financial elite. "If it goes down, I had nothing to do with it." As the clock struck midnight, Ali was in Washington, D.C., dining on beluga caviar, lobster, and foie gras. That saddened a lot of people. Ali makes his own decisions, but those decisions are made based on how information is presented to him. One can be forgiven for thinking that, had the options been explained differently to him, he would have chosen to serve as a different symbol that day.

The commercialization of Ali is also typified by the 2001 feature film that bore his name. The movie *Ali* represented a unique opportunity to depict its subject for generations, now and in the future, that didn't experience his magic. It cost the staggering sum of $105,000,000 to make and was backed by a multinational promotional campaign that cost tens of millions of dollars. But instead of being faithful to its subject, *Ali* rewrote history.

Ali featured countless factual inaccuracies for "dramatic purposes," as though Ali's life to date hasn't been dramatic enough. The screenplay was disjointed, and the film suffered from the hard reality that no one but Ali can play Ali. But the biggest problem with the movie was that it sanitized Ali and turned him into a virtual Disney character.

"I hated that film," says director Spike Lee. "It wasn't Ali."

"The movie was appalling," adds Robert Lipsyte, who for years covered Ali as a *New York Times* reporter. "They got the plastic covering on Elijah Muhammad's living-room furniture right, but that's about all."

"Will Smith playing Ali was an impersonation," adds Jerry Izenberg, "not a performance."

Also, in an effort to remove all of the warts from Ali's character, *Ali* the movie painted a portrait of its subject—and in the process, of America—that was flat-out wrong. Some of this sanitization, such as reducing Ali's profligate womanizing to a single meaningful relationship, is understandable. Ali's penchant for the opposite sex, while at odds with his public religious pronouncements, was not at the core of his public persona. But other omissions were far more damaging to the historical record and integrity of the film.

For example, Ali's cruelty toward Joe Frazier was completely ignored. In real life, Ali played the race card against Frazier in a particularly mean-spirited way. For the entertainment of white America, he labeled Joe as ugly and dumb. And at the same time, speaking to black America, he branded Frazier an Uncle Tom, turning him into an object of derision and scorn within the black community. The latter insult was particularly galling. Joe Frazier is a lot of things, not all of them good. But he's not an Uncle Tom. Yet to this day, there are people who think of him as a less-than-proud black man because of Ali's diatribes more than three decades ago.

"One of the many paradoxes about Ali," says historian Randy Roberts, "is that he embraced an ideology that disparaged white people; yet he was never cruel to white people, only blacks. Except for occasional humorous barbs, Ali's white opponents were treated with dignity and respect. But things got ugly with Floyd Patterson, Ernie Terrell, and Joe Frazier. And sure, Patterson and Terrell might have asked for it because of things they said. But Joe was innocent. And to deny the cruelty of what Ali did to Joe Frazier is to continue to be cruel to Joe."

In truth, it takes a certain amount of cruelty to be a great fighter. Let's not forget, Ali beat people up and inflicted brain damage on them as his livelihood and way of life for years. And the time when he was at his peak as a fighter coincided with the time when he was most openly angry at the circumstances he found.

Thus, the biggest problem with the film was not its portrayal of Ali's conduct but its misrepresentation of his thoughts. In an effort to create a simple conflict between good and evil (with Ali being good), the movie ignored the true nature of the Nation of Islam. Watching the film, the audience was left with the impression that Nation of Islam doctrine is Islam as practiced by more than one billion people around the world today. *Ali* depicted only that portion of Nation of Islam teachings that highlighted black pride, black self-awareness, and self-love.

Moreover, in promoting the view that America turned against Ali in the 1960s because he was a "Muslim"—as opposed to a member of the Nation of Islam—the makers of *Ali* fed into the dangerous view that America is "anti-Islam." The truth is, there were people who assailed Ali because they thought he was unpatriotic. There were people who assailed Ali because he was spouting a racist ideology or because they thought he was an "uppity" black man who didn't know his place. But Americans did not assail Ali because he was a

Muslim. Other public figures such as Lew Alcindor, who converted to orthodox Islam and changed his name to Kareem Abdul-Jabbar, were not vilified for their religious beliefs.

In sum, Ali is now being retroactively turned into a forerunner of Michael Jordan and Tiger Woods. "A bargain has been struck," says Robert Lipsyte. "Ali and the people around him get their money. And I'm glad Ali is making money. He's showing great gallantry in the face of his physical condition, and he never made what he should have made before. But the trade-off is, Ali is no longer threatening. He's safe; he's comfortable. He's another dangerous black man who white America has found a way to emasculate. You know, white America still hasn't figured out how to deal with powerful black male figures who don't play football or basketball other than to find ways to tame them and take away any real power and influence they might have. So the bottom line is, if we can control Muhammad Ali, it makes us more powerful. And at long last, we've brought Muhammad Ali under control."

Mike Marqusee, author of *Redemption Song: Muhammad Ali and the Spirit of the Sixties*, is in accord with Lipsyte and observes, "Ali's power in the third world grew precisely because he was a symbol of defiance against racism and the use of United States military power abroad. And those issues are very much alive today; so it means a lot to the powers that be if Ali can be used to suggest to the rest of the world that they aren't problems anymore. Governments and corporations have this incredible power to incorporate imagery and attach whatever meanings they choose to that imagery in pursuit of their goals. Nothing can take away Ali's past. It happened; it's part of history. But that history is now being plundered and deliberately obscured to sell commercial products and, more significantly, ideas. Ali is being reduced to serving as a mouthpiece for whatever ideas and products those with influence and power want to sell. And the people guiding him are letting it happen for narrow financial reasons."

"Most great athletes can sell Wheaties," notes Ramsey Clark. "But they can't impact upon social and political issues. It's very hard, if not impossible, to do both."

Clark's voice is significant. As Attorney General of the United

States, he oversaw as a matter of duty the 1967 criminal prosecution of Ali for refusing induction into the United States Army. However, he has long been aligned with liberal causes and has worked closely with Ali on a number of occasions.

"There's a common tactic among the dominant opinion-makers," says Clark. "They want to influence the population they're communicating with, so they transmit information selectively and create an image that's unreal but very powerful. On the one hand, they'll demonize their subject. Or in the other direction, they'll overlook the sins of someone they want to popularize and focus on the aspects of that person's life which reflect values they want to promote. It's a question of what those in power want to impose and consider safe. And what we have now in many of the depictions of Ali is the portrait of a man who is heroic, well-intentioned, and good—all of which he was and still is—but who is presented to us in an unreal artificial manner."

Ron Borges of the *Boston Globe* has followed Ali and the American scene for decades. "It's not uncommon for historical figures to slip out of focus when removed from their time by several generations," says Borges. "But this is something more. There's a deliberate distortion of what Ali's life has been like and what his impact on America really was. Maybe someone thinks that this sort of revisionism makes Ali more acceptable. But acceptable to whom and for what purpose other than selling products and making money? They're cutting out all the things that made him Ali. Frankly, I wonder sometimes what Ali is about these days other than making money. I know that, underneath the facade, Ali is still there. But to a lot of people, it's like he's a ghost. Twenty-year-olds today have no idea what Ali was about. As far as they're concerned, he's just another celebrity. That's what it has come to, and it steals Ali's true legacy."

Dave Kindred authored a number of ground-breaking stories about Ali for the *Atlanta Constitution* and *Washington Post*. "In the past," says Kindred, "there were reasons, a lot of them, for admiring and respecting Ali. Now you're asked to admire and respect him because he's a living saint. And I never thought of Ali as a saint. He was a rogue and a rebel, a guy with good qualities and flaws who stood for something. But now, it seems as though he stands for every-thing and nothing. All of the barbed edges have been filed down. His past is being rewritten. They're trying to remove any vestige of Ali that might make it harder to use him to sell automobiles or expensive watches or whatever other product he's endorsing at the moment. That, to me, is the heart of it. Ali today seems to be blatantly for sale. He's trotted around to high-profile events and events where he's paid large sums of money for being there, and often I find myself asking, 'What's he doing there?' I assume he enjoys it. I'm sure he likes the attention. His need for the crowd has always been there and he's entitled to the money. But the loss of Ali's voice is very sad. And I'm not talking about his physical voice, because the people around Ali have figured out a way to deal with his infirmities and still keep him center stage. I'm talking about content and hard edge and the challenge that attached to some of the things Ali said in the past. There was a time when Ali forced us to think about race and reli-gion and many of the other fundamental forces that affect our lives. He was right on some things and wrong on others, but the chal-lenge was always there. And that Ali is gone now, with the result that there's a whole new generation—two generations, actually—who know only the sanitized Ali, and that's very sad."

Jeffrey Sammons, a professor of African-American studies at NYU and author of *Beyond The Ring: The Role of Boxing in American Society,* is in accord. "What's happening to Ali now," says Sammons, "is typical of what has happened to so many black figures. It's a commodifica-tion and a trivialization. Maybe the idea is that, by embracing Ali as a society, we can feel good about having become more tolerant. We can tell ourselves that we're not like those bad people in the 1960s who took away Ali's title and his right to fight. But by not showing what Ali was, we're also not showing what American society was at that time. And if the rough edges on Ali are filed down, you have the revision of history in a very dangerous way. By distorting America's past, you make it impossible to understand the past. And if you can't understand the past, then you won't be able to under-stand the present or the future."

None of the above comments is intended to take away from Ali's greatness. Each of the speakers is a longtime admirer of Ali. Each of them would no doubt agree with the assessment of boxing maven Lou DiBella, who says, "In many respects, the way Ali is portrayed today is simply a reflection of how well loved he is and the fact that he's a great person. All of us are open to adoration and, in Ali's case, he deserves it. He's older, wiser, and mellower now than he was decades ago. He enjoys being who he is. And whatever good things he gets, he deserves them."

Still, Ali's legacy today is in danger of being protected in the same manner as the estate of Elvis Presley is protecting Elvis' image. New generations are born, and to them, Ali is more legend than reality, part of America's distant past.

Meanwhile, 2004 has brought more of the same. The year began with IBM, Gillette, and adidas featuring Ali in multinational commercial campaigns. Taschen Books published an Ali coffee-table tome bound in silk and Louis Vuitton leather that retails for $3,000 a copy, with a "special edition" that sells for $7,500. The book is entitled *GOAT*, which is an acronym for "Greatest of All Time" and also the name of Ali's personal company.

"I think it's significant," says Jerry Izenberg, "that the book is named after Ali's corporation and not Ali." Then Izenberg adds, "For those who didn't live through the 1960s, it takes some work to understand the true importance of Ali. And people are lazy; the media is lazy. No one wants to read and study. So they take the product that's given to them by IMG, Columbia Pictures, and others, and accept it whole cloth. The result is that, the further removed in time we become, the more Ali is distorted. And I get very angry about that, because the distortion of history breeds ignorance. If Ali isn't remembered as the person he truly was, we'll all be poorer. It will wipe out some very important lessons that America learned. Let's face it, most people today don't have a clue about Ali. They have no idea what Ali and the country went through in the 1960s. Ali isn't the same person now that he was then. Like most of us, he changed as he grew older. But I don't worry about the changes in Ali. I worry about the misperception of what Ali stood for. Ali can be all things to all people but, unless there's truth, it's worthless."

Ali in the 1960s stood for the proposition that principles matter; that equality among people is just and proper; that the war in

Vietnam was wrong. Every time he looked in the mirror and preened, "I'm so pretty," he was saying "black is beautiful" before it became fashionable to do so. Indeed, as early as March 1963, *Ebony* magazine declared, "Cassius Marcellus Clay—and this fact has evaded the sportswriting fraternity—is a blast furnace of racial pride. His is a pride that would never mask itself with skin lighteners and processed hair, a pride scorched with memories of a million little burns."

And Ali's role in spreading that pride has been testified to by others:

Arthur Ashe: "This man helped give an entire people a belief in themselves and the will to make themselves better."

Reggie Jackson: "Muhammad Ali gave me the gift of self-respect."

Hosea Williams: "Ali made you feel good about yourself. He made you feel so glad you are who you are; that God had made you black."

In sum, the experience of being black changed for millions of men and women because of Ali. But one of the reasons Ali had the impact he did was because there was an ugly edge to what he said. And by focusing on Ali's ring exploits and his refusal to serve in Vietnam, while at the same time covering up the true nature of Nation of Islam doctrine, the current keepers of Ali's legacy are losing sight of why he so enthralled and enraged segments of American society. And equally important, by rewriting history and making Ali out to be in the mainstream of the black civil rights movement, the revisionists demean Ali's personal struggle because they gloss over the extent to which he was cut off from mainstream support.

Thus, Ramsey Clark warns, "Legacies are important but they have to be true. The distortion of a legacy is a distortion of public truth and a disservice to history, as are all distortions of values and character."

Ali himself once recalled, "For three years, up until I fought Sonny Liston, I'd sneak into Nation of Islam meetings through the back door. I didn't want people to know I was there. I was afraid, if they knew, I wouldn't be allowed to fight for the title. Later on, I learned to stand up for my beliefs."

Ali's views have changed since then, but he is unrepentant regarding what he once believed. "Elijah Muhammad was a good man," Ali has said, "even if he wasn't the Messenger of God we thought he was. Not everything he said was right, but everyone in the Nation of Islam loved him because he carried what was best for us in his heart. Elijah taught us to be independent, to clean ourselves up, to be proud and healthy. He stressed the bad things the white man did to us so we could get free and strong. If you look at what our people were like then, a lot of us didn't have self-respect. We didn't have anything after being in America for hundreds of years. Elijah Muhammad was trying to lift us up and get our people out of the gutter. I think he was wrong when he talked about white devils, but part of what he did was make people feel it was good to be black. So I'm not apologizing for what I believed."

It's the ultimate irony then, that so many of the people shaping Ali's legacy today are "spin-doctoring" with regard to his beliefs. Ali stood up for his convictions and sacrificed a great deal for them. Indeed, in a recent commercial for IBM's Linux system, Ali speaks the words, "Speak your mind; don't back down." So why hide the true nature of what Ali's principles were?

Also, it should be said that, in 2005, there's a particularly compelling reason to mourn the lost legacy of Muhammad Ali.

We live in an age marked by horrific divisions amongst the world's cultures and religions. If we are to avoid increasingly violent assaults and possibly a nuclear holocaust, the people of the world must learn to understand others with alien beliefs, find the humanity in their enemies, and embrace that which is good in those they abhor.

Muhammad Ali is the ideal messenger for this cause. He is a man who once preached an ideology that was anathema to most Americans, an ideology that he himself now rejects in significant measure. Yet America has found the humanity in Ali, embraced the good in him, and taken him into its collective heart. And vice versa.

Also, it should be noted that, were he so inclined, Ali is still capable of influencing public debate. All he would need to say is two words regarding the current war in Iraq: "*It's wrong!*" That wouldn't dictate what people think, but it would have a significant impact on what a lot of people thought about. However, instead, Ali has held to the theme advised by those around him and advanced when he was asked about al-Qaeda in June 2002.

"I dodge those questions," Ali told David Frost on *HBO Reel Sports.* "I've opened up businesses across the country, selling products, and I don't want to say nothing and, not knowing what I'm doing, not [being] qualified, say the wrong thing and hurt my businesses and things I'm doing."

It's hard to imagine Muhammad Ali in the 1960s declining to comment on war and racism for fear that it would hurt his business ventures.

Great men are considered great, not only because of what they achieve, but also because of the road they travel to reach their final destination. Sanitizing Muhammad Ali and rounding off the rough edges of his journey is a disservice both to history and to Ali himself. Rather than cultivate historical amnesia, we should cherish the memory of Ali as a warrior and as a gleaming symbol of defiance against an unjust social order when he was young.

Cassius Clay swings at Australia's Tony Madigan in
the light-heavyweight semifinals of the 1960 Olympics.

Muhammad Ali's Ring Record

Professional Record: 56 wins, 5 losses, 37 KOs

OLYMPIC RECORD

August 30, 1960	Yan Becaus (Belgium)	KO 2
September 1, 1960	Genadiy Schatkov (USSR)	W 3
September 3, 1960	Tony Madigan (Australia)	W 3
September 5, 1960	Zbigniew Pietrzykowki (Poland)	W 3
	(Won Olympic Light-Heavyweight Gold Medal)	

PROFESSIONAL FIGHTS

October 29, 1960	Tunney Hunsaker	Louisville, KY	W 6
December 27, 1960	Herb Siler	Miami Beach, FL	KO 4
January 17, 1961	Tony Esperti	Miami Beach, FL	KO 3
February 7, 1961	Jim Robinson	Miami Beach, FL	KO 1
February 21, 1961	Donnie Fleeman	Miami Beach, FL	KO 7
April 19, 1961	Lamar Clark	Louisville, KY	KO 2
June 26, 1961	Duke Sabedong	Las Vegas, NV	W 10
July 22, 1961	Alonzo Johnson	Louisville, KY	W 10
October 7, 1961	Alex Miteff	Louisville, KY	KO 6
November 28, 1961	Willi Besmanoff	Louisville, KY	KO 7
February 19, 1962	Sonny Banks	New York, NY	KO 4
March 28, 1962	Don Warner	Miami Beach, FL	KO 4
April 23, 1962	George Logan	Los Angeles, CA	KO 6
May 19, 1962	Billy Daniels	New York, NY	KO 7
July 20, 1962	Alejandro Lavorante	Los Angeles, CA	KO 5

213

November 15, 1962	Archie Moore	Los Angeles, CA	KO 4
January 24, 1963	Charlie Powell	Pittsburgh, PA	KO 3
March 13, 1963	Doug Jones	New York, NY	W 10
June 18, 1963	Henry Cooper	London, England	KO 5
February 25, 1964	Sonny Liston	Miami Beach, FL	KO 7
(Won World Heavyweight Championship)			
May 25, 1965	Sonny Liston	Lewiston, ME	KO 1
(Retained World Heavyweight Championship)			
November 22, 1965	Floyd Patterson	Las Vegas, NV	KO 12
(Retained World Heavyweight Championship)			
March 29, 1966	George Chuvalo	Toronto, Canada	W 15
(Retained World Heavyweight Championship)			
May 21, 1966	Henry Cooper	London, England	KO 6
(Retained World Heavyweight Championship)			
August 6, 1966	Brian London	London, England	KO 3
(Retained World Heavyweight Championship)			
September 10, 1966	Karl Mildenberger	Frankfurt, Germany	KO 12
(Retained World Heavyweight Championship)			
November 14, 1966	Cleveland Williams	Houston, TX	KO 3
(Retained World Heavyweight Championship)			
February 6, 1967	Ernie Terrell	Houston, TX	W 15
(Retained World Heavyweight Championship)			
March 22, 1967	Zora Folley	New York, NY	KO 7
(Retained World Heavyweight Championship)			
October 26, 1970	Jerry Quarry	Atlanta, GA	KO 3
December 7, 1970	Oscar Bonavena	New York, NY	KO 15
March 8, 1971	Joe Frazier	New York, NY	L 15
(Challenged for World Heavyweight Championship)			
July 26, 1971	Jimmy Ellis	Houston, TX	KO 12
November 17, 1971	Buster Mathis	Houston, TX	W 12
December 26, 1971	Jurgen Blin	Zurich, Switzerland	KO 7
April 1, 1972	Mac Foster	Tokyo, Japan	W 15
May 1, 1972	George Chuvalo	Vancouver, Canada	W 12
June 27, 1972	Jerry Quarry	Las Vegas, NV	KO 7
July 19, 1972	Al Lewis	Dublin, Ireland	KO 11
September 20, 1972	Floyd Patterson	New York, NY	KO 7
November 21, 1972	Bob Foster	Stateline, NV	KO 8
February 14, 1973	Joe Bugner	Las Vegas, NV	W 12
March 31, 1973	Ken Norton	San Diego, CA	L 12
September 10, 1973	Ken Norton	Los Angeles, CA	W 12
October 21, 1973	Rudi Lubbers	Jakarta, Indonesia	W 12

January 28, 1974	Joe Frazier	New York, NY	W 12
October 30, 1974	George Foreman	Kinshasa, Zaire	KO 8
	(Won World Heavyweight Championship)		
March 24, 1975	Chuck Wepner	Cleveland, OH	KO 15
	(Retained World Heavyweight Championship)		
May 16, 1975	Ron Lyle	Las Vegas, NV	KO 11
	(Retained World Heavyweight Championship)		
June 30, 1975	Joe Bugner	Kuala Lumpur, Malaysia	W 15
	(Retained World Heavyweight Championship)		
October 1, 1975	Joe Frazier	Quezon City, Philippines	KO 14
	(Retained World Heavyweight Championship)		
February 20, 1976	Jean Pierre Coopman	San Juan, Puerto Rico	KO 5
	(Retained World Heavyweight Championship)		
April 30, 1976	Jimmy Young	Landover, MD	W 15
	(Retained World Heavyweight Championship)		
May 24, 1976	Richard Dunn	Munich, Germany	KO 5
	(Retained World Heavyweight Championship)		
September 28, 1976	Ken Norton	New York, NY	W 15
	(Retained World Heavyweight Championship)		
May 16, 1977	Alfredo Evangelista	Landover, MD	W 15
	(Retained World Heavyweight Championship)		
September 29, 1977	Earnie Shavers	New York, NY	W 15
	(Retained World Heavyweight Championship)		
February 15, 1978	Leon Spinks	Las Vegas, NV	L 15
	(Lost World Heavyweight Championship)		
September 15, 1978	Leon Spinks	New Orleans, LA	W15
	(Won World Heavyweight Championship)		
October 2, 1980	Larry Holmes	Las Vegas, NV	L KO 11
	(Challenged for World Heavyweight Championship)		
December 11, 1981	Trevor Berbick	Nassau, Bahamas	L 10

Index

Page numbers in italics refer to photographs.

Praise for Thomas Hauser's
Muhammad Ali: His Life and Times

"This is an important slice of American history...It should be required reading in every high school and college."
— *New York Daily News*

"A feast for fans. This composite portrait bristles with insights, jabs and tributes."
— *Publishers Weekly*

"This is by far the best book ever written about Muhammad Ali, and one of the best ever written about a celebrity-entertainment-controversial figure."
— *Los Angeles Sentinel*

"Ali was bigger than boxing, and so is this book." — *The Nation*

"Hauser's skill gives this rich and absorbing portrait a flow and drive....and his training as a lawyer offers a precision that creates a new foundation for all future Ali scholarship." — *Los Angeles Times*

"*Muhammad Ali: His Life and Times* is a magnificent book (about) a life that needs to be understood whether you care a whit about boxing or not."
— *Boston Globe*

"The most significant boxing book ever written...Read this extraordinary work."
— *Ring Magazine*

"What you come away with at the end of this ambitious oral history is all you ever wanted to know about Muhammad Ali."

— *Chicago Tribune*

"We now have a definitive biography of Muhammad Ali, who transcended sports as no other athlete ever has."

— *The New York Times*

"Thomas Hauser has produced the definitive extraordinary story of an extraordinary man."

— *Los Angeles Daily News*

"The book is fascinating from start to finish."

— *The American Spectator*

"I doubt that we shall ever see a more comprehensive portrait of this extraordinary athlete."

— *The Sporting News*

"At last! This is the book that we have been waiting for."

— *Boxing News*

"Hauser has come up with a superb book."

— *London Times*

"Hauser's approach has been so comprehensive, his research so thorough, that the result is a tour de force."

— *London Observer*

"Thomas Hauser's riveting biography of Muhammad Ali is triumphant and harrowing at one and the same time."

— *London Guardian*

"A monumental achievement."

— *London Daily Telegraph*

"This is the best of the books about Ali; the most thorough, honest, well-researched, well-organized book out there."

— *Philadelphia Daily News*